Whiter Shades of Pale

THE STUFF WHITE PEOPLE LIKE,

Whiter

COAST TO COAST,

Shades

FROM SEATTLE'S SWEATERS

# of Pale

TO MAINE'S MICROBREWS

Christian Lander

RANDOM HOUSE TRADE PAPERBACKS NEW YORK

This book is dedicated to everyone who ever forwarded, emailed, posted, or laughed at an entry on Stuff White People Like. Thank you.

A Random House Trade Paperback Original

Copyright © 2010 by Christian Lander

Published in the United States
by Random House Trade Paperbacks,
an imprint of The Random House Publishing Group,
a division of Random House, Inc., New York.

RANDOM HOUSE TRADE PAPERBACKS and colophon
are trademarks of Random House, Inc.

Some of the material in this book originally appeared,
occasionally in different form, in the blog Stuff White People Like
(http://stuffwhitepeoplelike.com).

All illustration credits can be found on page 233.

Library of Congress Cataloging-in-Publication Data

Lander, Christian.
Whiter shades of pale: the stuff white people like, coast to coast, from Seattle's sweaters to
Maine's microbrews / by Christian Lander.
p. cm.
ISBN 978-0-8129-8206-0
1. Whites—United States—Humor. 2. American wit and humor. 3. Race awareness—
Humor. I. Title.
PN6231.W444L36 2010
818'.602—dc22 2010035303

Printed in the United States of America

www.atrandom.com

9 8 7 6 5 4 3 2 1

Introduction

When I began Stuff White People Like back in January 2008, my knowledge of white people was limited mostly to my twenty-nine years of being white. But I had traveled a bit and spent four years in graduate school, so I was still in a pretty good position to observe the habits of the modern white individual.

So I started writing about them. Little did I know that there would be so many people interested in white people and how to exploit them for personal gain. Things went well. I wrote a book, I went on a few talk shows, and for a while I thought I was a man who knew all he could know about being white.

Then I went on a book tour.

My travels took me to magical places like Madison, Wisconsin; Austin, Texas; Portland, Oregon; and Chapel Hill, North Carolina. It became painfully evident that I still had a lot to learn about white people.

There were handicrafts beyond my wildest dreams: "Another hemp hacky sack! Thanks, Boulder, Colorado!" During my journeys I was introduced to many exotic grains that I could now eat in place of processed flour and that would somehow fix everything that was wrong with me. "You're right, I do feel more centered after eating this quinoa."

It was an eye-opening experience that helped me realize that as much as all white people are the same, in many ways they are slightly, superficially different.

But then again, there are few things that white people like more than slight, superficial differences. For proof, ask one about the difference between punk and post-punk and you're likely to see your afternoon evaporate with a drawn-out pointless argument.

So I've set out to continue finding all those things that bind white people together in unity, but this time I want to take it further. I want to take it to the independent coffeeshops of the college towns in the Midwest, the music festivals in rural Tennessee, the bicycle collectives in Los Angeles, and many more places.

Stuff White People Like is going regional.*

*If your city isn't in here, I apologize. But remember, we're all pretty much the same. Also, maybe you should consider a move to Brooklyn or Portland; every other white person is doing the same thing.

Whiter Shades of Pale

Red Sox hat.

Democratic Party gear everywhere.

Harvard sweatshirt. Yet for some reason they are awkward about telling you they went to Harvard ("I went to school in Cambridge").

Boston, Massachusetts

- **Overview** White people in Boston are very proud of their blue-collar roots. However, for many of them, two generations is as close as they will ever get to a job requiring manual labor. This also extends to the many Bostonians who will still send their white children to public school, provided that public school is Boston Latin. Boston is also home to three alternative newsweeklies that provide many young writers with jobs that don't pay enough to make rent. The Boston white person can also be found throughout rural New England, but this breed is special, having cast off the shackles of the workaday world to begin a small organic microbrewery, creamery, or farm.

- **Strengths** *Mayflower* relatives give them low-numbered license plates; can hold liquor.

- **Weaknesses** Baseball-induced depression; movies about Irish gangsters.

- **Secret Shame** They don't really like the Dropkick Murphys.

1 Ivy League

The Ivy League is expensive, exclusive, and located in the Northeast and has campuses featuring beautiful, actual ivy-covered buildings. All these things are beloved by white people, so logically it would seem that they all love the Ivy League. But this is not true!

White people have a tortured relationship with the Ivy League, and if you broach the subject in the wrong way you can offend and even anger a white person.

But before getting into the more nuanced aspects of the subject, it's important to know that all white people believe they are intelligent enough and have the work ethic required to attend an Ivy League school. The only reason they did not actually attend one is that they chose not to participate in the "dog and pony  show" required to gain acceptance. White people also like to believe that they were not born into a privileged (enough) family for the coveted legacy admission. This should always be at the back of your mind as you discuss the Ivy League with a white person.

Once you have determined that a white person did not attend an Ivy League school, you should try to give them the opportunity to explain why their school was actually a superior educational experience. Some easy ways to do this: mention grade inflation, professors who value research over teaching, or high tuition costs. Any one of these will set a white person off on a multiminute rant.

When they have reached the end of their defense about why they chose the "right" school, you should say, "I knew a whole bunch of people who went to Harvard and none of them work as hard or are as smart as you." This is a very effective technique for gaining acceptance among white people, since they need constant reassurance that they are smart and that they made the right choice with their life.

If you actually attended an Ivy League school, you will be seen as a threat, so prepare for a lot of questions from white people. They will constantly ask about how much work you had, the type of students at the school, the professors, your dorm room, and your reading lists, and they will try so hard to figure out your SAT score. They desperately need a source of comparison so that they can determine if you are actually smarter than them. In fact, the only way to stop this line of questioning is to imply that you only got in because of your minority status. Once you say that, white people will stop feeling threatened, since they can now believe they too would have been accepted to an Ivy League school if they were a minority. It also gives them a personal story about the effectiveness of affirmative action.

White people also like to call their school "the Harvard of the [insert region or athletic conference]." Do not challenge this; it will ruin their confidence.

2 Conan O'Brien

The news that Conan O'Brien would be replaced by Jay Leno caused white people to erupt with rage and hostility. You might have expected them to lash out and do something about it, like take to the streets or write letters to NBC to voice their dissatisfaction with the network. But no, white people solved this problem the way that they solved the election crisis in Iran: through Facebook and Twitter updates. In 2009, millions of white people took thirty-five seconds to turn their Twitter profiles green, and consequently sent a very powerful message to the leaders of Iran. Their message was that they wanted their friends to know that they would stop at nothing to ensure freedom and democracy for the Iranian people. Thanks in large part to that effort, Iran is now a functioning democratic paradise (as far as white people know). With that issue settled, white people launched a similar campaign for Conan that is sure to have similar results.

It is not hard to understand why white people love Conan O'Brien. He embodies so many of the things they already like: Ivy League schools, Red Hair, the Boston Red Sox, Self-Deprecating Humor, *The Simpsons*, and Bad Memories of High School (likely, but not confirmed). Seeing him on TV five nights a week gives white people who still have televisions a comforting sense of community.

If your plan is to try to use Conan O'Brien as a way to get white people to become more interested in you, then it is imperative that you understand a few key rules. First, all white people love "the Masturbating Bear." If you don't know what this is, do not worry. Just proclaim your love for the character, and the white person you are talking to will simply fill in the rest. Second, all white people believe that Andy Richter never should have left the show in the first place. And finally, you should do your best to develop a "Triumph the Insult Comic Dog" impression. All white people already have one, so you might as well try to fit in. Complete these steps and watch your friendship with white people become considerably smoother.

Now, the biggest and most important thing to remember is to never, under any circumstance, bring up a Conan O'Brien sketch or joke that has taken place in the last five years. You will be met with only blank stares. For you see, while white people will fiercely support Conan O'Brien in any public forum, they always fail to support him in the only way that actually helps—by watching his show.

Note: Under no circumstance should you ever mention that you prefer Jay Leno. This might cause white people to think you have the same taste in humor as the wrong kind of white people, or worse, their parents.

3 Single-Malt Scotch

There is no getting around the subject: white people love alcohol. From their refined tastes in French wine to their fervent consumption of Maine's microbrews, booze makes up a very important part of white culture. But many white people soon realize there are only so many beers that one can drink, and that being an expert on wine is almost impossible. Currently the most realistic way for a white person to look like a wine expert is to look at a restaurant's wine list and

then promptly order a bottle of a cheap—but not the cheapest—bottle on the menu. Advanced white people will pretend they recognize and enjoy this moderately priced bottle of wine.

With beer snobbery mastered and wine snobbery all but abandoned, white people were forced to try to find a new alcohol for snobbery. The process of elimination is a fairly simple procedure. First, any alcohol that's mentioned by a rapper is immediately cast aside. Not just brands, but the alcohol itself. This is not because white people have any prejudice against rappers. Quite the opposite, in fact: their prejudice is simply against other white people who do what rappers tell them.

Increased sales of Grey Goose, Patrón, Hennessy, and Cristal have effectively erased any real opportunity for white people to participate in snobbery about each respective beverage. To a white person there could be no greater shame than waiting in line at a liquor store and having a twenty-year-old frat boy say to them:

> "Oh what? You're on that 'yak too?"
> "This is a Hine Triomphe, perhaps the world's finest—"
> "I'm on that Hennessy!"

Even the possibility of this exchange has sent white people, especially white men, scrambling for an alcoholic beverage to set them apart from these wrong kinds of white people. What they found was single-malt scotch.

It has everything a white person could want. It's got European heritage, it's expensive, college-age white people avoid it, and perhaps most important, crotchety old white men love it. The latter point is especially important, since you should understand that white people, for whatever reason, are generally inclined to like or force themselves to like anything that angry, intelligent, old white men enjoy: sweaters, jazz, things made from wood, books, records, and complaining about how everything is terrible now.

4 Complaining About the Death of Print Media

White people are expert complainers. Witness the events that transpire after they are served a dish they didn't order in a restaurant. But that type of complaining is done by all people. No, what white people are best at is complaining without being willing to actually do anything about the problem; see Conan O'Brien, Iran, Oil Spills, Air Pollution, Tuna Depletion, and any problem that would require them to make a sacrifice of time, money, or sushi dining experiences.

But in recent years, the biggest issue that has been bugging white people to the point of complaint but not action has been the death of print media. Bring up any newspaper and white people will begin saying how they fear for a world with no daily newspaper and that we will all suffer as professional journalists wither away and are replaced with silly blogs that have no importance.

This love of the print media comes from two places. The first is that all white people like to believe that they spend the majority of their news-consuming time reading the stories that matter and make a difference. Whether this is true is irrelevant, but it is a good way to appear smart to white people. Say something like "I can't believe no one is getting upset

about what the city government is doing right now. It's like no one read that amazing piece in the paper." The white person will agree with you and respect your news acumen.

Second, white people fear the death of the print media because deep down all white people want to believe that it's possible to make a living as a freelance writer. Of course, this is perhaps the biggest lie in white culture, pushing out such favorites as "I'm going to write a novel" and "I'll be fine for retirement if I start saving when I'm forty."

Of course, when you ask the white person if they actually subscribe to a daily newspaper, they will say that they get the Sunday *New York Times*. Which is a bit like saying you sponsor a child in Africa but only give enough money for him to eat on Sunday.

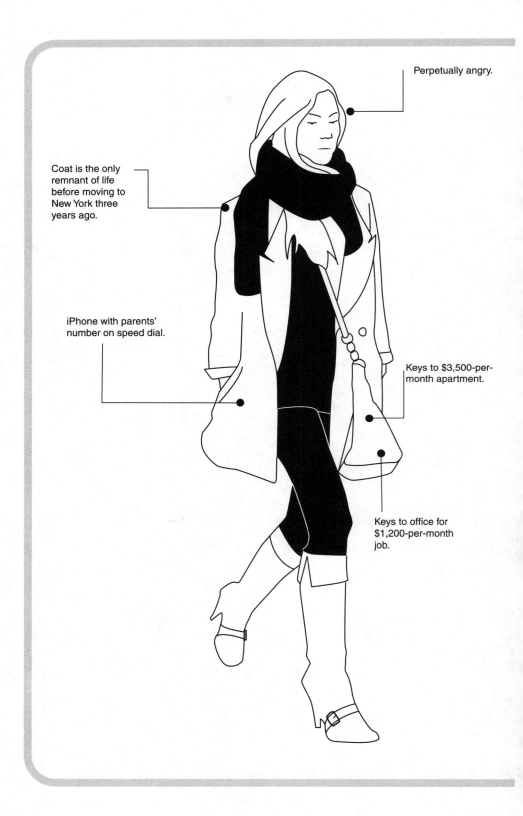

Perpetually angry.

Coat is the only remnant of life before moving to New York three years ago.

iPhone with parents' number on speed dial.

Keys to $3,500-per-month apartment.

Keys to office for $1,200-per-month job.

New York, New York

- **Overview** The New York City resident is one of the most envied white people in the entire world. Their access to art galleries, restaurants, public transit, and pools of hobo urine is second to none. Fiercely proud of their city, all New Yorkers consider themselves to be the last one in. That is to say, everyone who moved to New York after them made the city a considerably worse place to live and thus are not considered "real New Yorkers."

- **Strengths** Can get you into places that don't exist; able to survive in small spaces.

- **Weaknesses** Cannot go fifteen minutes without telling you they live in New York. Also driving.

- **Secret Shame** Actually from Ohio.

5 Unpaid Internships

Throughout most of the world, when a person works long hours without pay, it is referred to as "slavery" or "forced labor." For white people this process is referred to as an internship and is considered to be an essential stage in white development.

The concept of working for little or no money under a mentor has been around for centuries in the form of apprenticeship programs. Young people eager to learn a trade would spend time working under a master craftsman to learn a skill that would eventually lead to an increase in the intern's own material wealth.

Using this logic you would assume that the most sought-after internships would be in areas that lead to the greatest financial reward. Young white people, however, prefer internships that put them on the path for careers that will generally result in a *decrease* of material wealth (at least when compared to the wealth accumulated by their parents).

For example, if you present a white nineteen-year-old with the choice of spending the summer earning $15 an hour as a plumber's apprentice or making $0 answering phones at Acme Production Company, they will always choose the latter. In fact, the only way to get the white person to choose the plumbing option would be to convince them that it was leading toward an end-of-summer pipe art installation.

White people view the unpaid internship as their foot in the door to such high-profile low-paying career fields as journalism, film, politics, art, nonprofits, and anything associated with a museum. Any white person who takes an internship outside these industries is either the wrong type of white person or a law student. There are no exceptions.

If all goes according to plan, an internship will end with an offer of a job that pays $24,000 per year and consists entirely of the same tasks they were recently doing for free. In fact, the transition to full-time status results in the addition of only one new responsibility: feeling superior to the new interns.

When all is said and done, the internship process serves the white community in many ways. First, it helps train the next generation of freelance writers, museum curators, and director's assistants. But second, and more important, internships teach white children how to complain about being poor.

So when a white person tells you about their unpaid internship at *The New Yorker*, it's not a good idea to point out how the cost of rent and food will essentially mean that they are *paying* for the right to make photocopies. Instead it's best to say, "You earned it." They will not get the joke.

6 Foreign Accents

When a white person sees something that is commonly available, they are often on the lookout for a way to make it seem slightly different. This allows them to stand out from the crowd, but not so much so that they might alienate other white people. Common examples include ironic facial hair, a Mac laptop with stickers on it, or an ethnic spouse or child. The ability to be just different enough is considered very attractive to white people, and over the past century nothing has attracted more white people than an accent.

Before delving into the reasons behind the popularity of accents, it's important to understand the system white people apply in determining whether an accent is sexy. For the most part, accents are only considered arousing if they come as a surprise. For example, if a white person encounters a Chinese person with a Chinese accent, that will not be considered particularly impressive. But if they encounter a Chinese person with a Swedish or Australian accent, that person will immediately become a crush object. For further evidence, ask any white person for their opinion on a successful black actor with a British accent.

When it comes to white people with accents, these same rules apply. There are few things more enjoyable to white people than meeting someone who appears to be exactly like them in every way except for their possession of an accent and a foreign passport. The latter is especially important, as it fuels every white person's dream of dual citizenship, preferably between the United States and a European Union country. (In a pinch, Australia or Canada can be substituted for the U.S., but not for Europe.) Within minutes of meeting this foreign individual, most white people will have at least one fantasy involving a scenario where they can say, "Well, we have dual citizen-

ship, so we're thinking about raising the children in Europe."

Of course, all of this presupposes that the person with the accent is of the opposite sex. An accented individual of the same sex may be considered a mortal enemy by most white people due to their unfair advantage in the white dating scene. Much like the competition for private schools, universities, and unpaid internships, the battle for acceptable spouses in the world of white people is cutthroat. And in the social-sexual rankings of white people, the right accent can compensate for a graduate degree, up to $40,000 a year in income, and bad teeth.

In the event that you find yourself competing with an accented person for a potential mate, it's best advised that you give up immediately or contact your local immigration enforcement office. These are your only options.

7 British Slang

The vocabulary of white people is constantly evolving. From actually saying Internet shorthand (OMG!) to trying to incorporate terms they read in *Wired* magazine, white people are always adding to their personal dictionaries. But these are both fairly recent developments. The one area that white people are always looking to co-opt is slang. Of course, nothing will ever top white people's love for African-American slang, but that's not to say they are afraid to borrow from other areas. In recent years, no area of slang has seen a larger spike in growth than British.

The use of British slang in everyday conversation says so much about the person using it. Not only does it imply that they have likely done a study abroad in the U.K.; it also suggests that their cable package includes BBC America. Within white culture, an affinity for British programming that has no chance of ever crossing over to America is seen as a very desirable thing indeed. For proof just ask any white person about *The Mighty Boosh* or *Garth Marenghi's Darkplace*.

By far and away the biggest reason white people start talking with British slang is the films of Guy Ritchie or *Trainspotting*. It is scientifically impossible for a white person to watch the first half of *Lock, Stock and Two Smoking Barrels* and not start using words like *shite* and *wanker*.

If you have any familiarity with British slang, it is essential that you keep your mouth shut around white people. It has been proven that British slang expression spreads faster than chlamydia among a group of white people.

If you do not believe this, there is a simple test you can perform. Before leaving a group situation simply say the words "Cheers, mate" instead of "Goodbye." Within twenty-four hours, emails written to you will end with that expression, and the next day at work will sound like you've stepped into the worst Cockney pub in the world.

8 Anthony Bourdain

One look at Anthony Bourdain's life accomplishments and it's no surprise that white people like him: famous chef, bestselling author, and television host who flies around the world eating local and exotic foods. He is truly a hero to white people everywhere.

In each episode of his TV show he travels to a new city and a guide instantly whisks him away to a restaurant or food stall that is proclaimed to be for locals only. Bourdain eats something that some people might consider to be gross, then proceeds to spend the next ten minutes complaining about tourists who only want to eat at chain restaurants.

This not only makes him feel better about pretending that the salted gallbladder he just ate was actually delicious, it also reminds the white people watching the show that they are better than everyone else. There hasn't been a show this reaffirming to white people since *Seinfeld*.

During the show he is also fond of talking about how he hates when too many white people start eating at a local ethnic restaurant. Which makes sense considering he's doing a show that specifically directs white people to these very establishments.

But the part of the show that fills white people with the most glee is when he goes to a very expensive high-end restaurant run by one of his friends. This is important because all white people respect high-end restaurants and all have elaborate fantasies about one day being able to eat at one. And there is the great value of this show.

Begin discussing *No Reservations* with a white person and try to steer the conversation toward a restaurant that Bourdain went to in Europe. Then use the following script.

> "If I can get a reservation, I'm going to Spain and I'm eating at elBulli."
>
> "How much is it?"
>
> "About four hundred euro per person, not including wine or the flight."
>
> "So my kid is selling candy bars to raise money for his school; can I get you to buy some?"

If the white person immediately caves and agrees to help out, then you have won a small victory. But the larger prize comes if they try to pretend they are broke.

If the white person rebuffs you, all you need to say is "So you have a few thousand dollars to spend on foie gras and truffles, but not ten bucks to help out some kids at *public* school? Class act, Josh."

Your child will be the top fund-raiser at your school. Or you will have made enough in false school candy bar sales to take a trip to elBulli.

9 Nannies

Raising a white child is extremely time-consuming. They have so many activities, cultural immersion programs, sports, language classes, and supplemental educational classes, and that doesn't include the time it takes to actually raise the child. For a white person to accomplish all of this they would need superhuman abilities or just have to make some personal sacrifices, both equally impossible to white people.

So to help manage this incredible task, white people hire nannies to help raise their children. When both parents work, a nanny becomes extremely important in child care. But wait, aren't there men and women who don't work but still have a nanny? Of course!

Just because you don't have a job doesn't mean you aren't busy. In fact, white people are regarded as the best in the world at looking busy while doing nothing. This is an important technique developed by white people over many years of trying to find a way to avoid returning awkward phone calls.

When it comes to hiring a nanny, there are a lot of rules. White nannies are generally seen as problematic. Since most of them are young Europeans or American women looking for an artistic career in a city, they pose a sexual threat to the recent mother. Additionally, with white nannies comes the fear that they will abandon the children if they find something better to do. This last fear is especially pronounced in white parents because it's exactly what they just did.

Instead, white people prize older foreign women. Their popularity is due to a number of factors. First, white people like hiring nannies who have children who are grown up. Or at least older than fourteen: that makes them feel better about essentially hiring someone to neglect their own children. Also, foreign women might teach the white child a new language. And finally, most foreign women who work as nannies have lived a long life of hard work and devotion to others, two skills that cannot be taught by white parents.

If you're invited to a Mother's Day party it is strongly recommended that you get a gift for the mother. Showing up with a gift for the nanny and saying, "What? She's the one doing all the work!" is considered to be poor form—though an excellent first step in poaching a nanny.

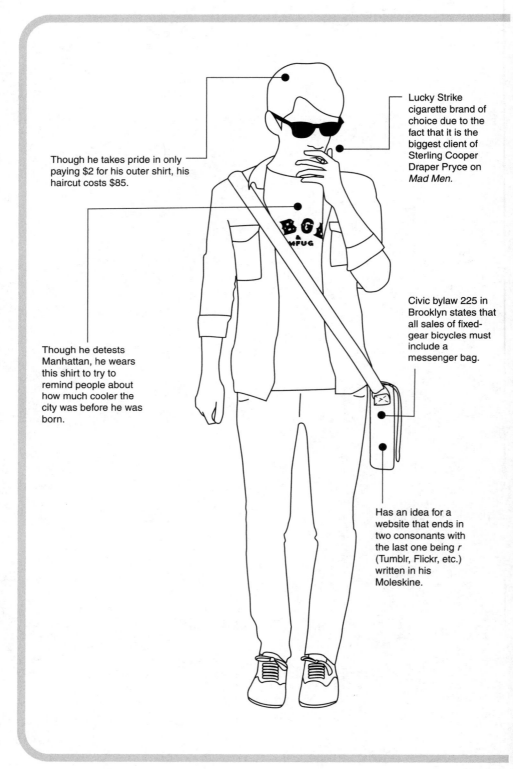

Though he takes pride in only paying $2 for his outer shirt, his haircut costs $85.

Lucky Strike cigarette brand of choice due to the fact that it is the biggest client of Sterling Cooper Draper Pryce on *Mad Men*.

Though he detests Manhattan, he wears this shirt to try to remind people about how much cooler the city was before he was born.

Civic bylaw 225 in Brooklyn states that all sales of fixed-gear bicycles must include a messenger bag.

Has an idea for a website that ends in two consonants with the last one being *r* (Tumblr, Flickr, etc.) written in his Moleskine.

Brooklyn, New York

- **Overview** The Brooklyn variety of white person is perhaps the coolest type of white person in America. They can be identified by their amazingly expensive bicycle, their disdain for Manhattan, and their unwavering belief that living in Brooklyn makes them a part of an ethnic community. The female version of the species is almost certainly a photographer, aspiring restaurant owner, or artist, while the male version is mostly made up of writers named Jonathan.

- **Strengths** Knows a lot about music, bicycles, food, and art.

- **Weaknesses** Knows a lot about music, bicycles, food, and art.

- **Secret Shame** Once enjoyed a meal at the Red Lobster in Times Square.

10 Funny or Ironic Tattoos

When you think about tattoo parlors, it conjures up images of sailors, gang members, hepatitis, and spring break. All of these are things that white people do not like, except for sailors, but that only counts if they were sailing before Vietnam. Yet in spite of this, more and more of the right white people are getting tattoos.

But do not make the mistake of thinking that white people like all tattoos. In fact, they loathe a great number of them, including

- anything with an American flag or eagle
- references to military service
- tribal armbands
- white heritage imagery
- faces of children, spouses, or dead people
- tattoos with more than one color

For a white person, getting a tattoo is a major step in their life since it presupposes that their taste at this given moment is good enough to sustain them for the rest of their lives. Needless to say, this is a near impossible task. This is why you don't see a lot of white people with R.E.M. or Strokes tattoos.

White people can only get tattoos of the only thing that they are guaranteed to like in five years; therefore, it is a very short list. But there are two things that will never go out of style with white people: humor and irony.

An ironic/funny tat can come in many forms: a piece of bacon, old Nintendo characters, mustaches on the side of their finger, or Asian characters that say something funny and self-aware like "dim sum," "chicken fried rice," or "I can't read Chinese."

The Chinese or Japanese character is an interesting case study about the dangers of getting a tattoo with a personal meaning. You see, about fifteen years ago these were considered to be acceptable. Then the wrong kind of white people started getting tattoos of sentences like "Trust no one" or single words like *beauty*, *truth*, or *endurance*. To make a more modern analogy, it would be like the Arcade Fire being featured on a Jock Jams CD.

White people learned their lesson.

A white person with the right kind of tattoo is generally very popular within the white community, since they have shown a demonstrated commitment to irony, humor, and in some cases, self-deprecation.

If you find yourself competing socially with one of them, there are a few things you can do in order to defeat them.

Your saving grace is the fact that white people not only enjoy getting funny/ironic tattoos, but they really enjoy talking about them, too! Therefore, it is essential that you already have two or three clever tattoo ideas ready to drop into a conversation.

"Yeah, that finger mustache is pretty cool, but a lot of people have it. [Note: This is the meanest thing you can say.] I'm thinking about getting a tattoo of a doughnut around my belly button or a picture of a hamburger on my forearm so I can order food when I'm in Japan."

Your conversation partner will likely then tell you about the clever tattoos that they have been thinking of, and before you know it they will have forgotten all about your competition.

11 Moleskine Notebooks

Since all white people consider themselves to be "creative," they are constantly in need of products and accessories that will allow them to capture their thoughts in a stylish manner. One of the more popular products in recent years has been the Moleskine notebook.

This particular type of notebook is very expensive and was quite popular with writers and artists in the olden days. Needless to say, these are two qualities that are highly coveted in the white community. In fact, it's a good rule of thumb to know that white people like anything that old writers and artists liked: typewriters, journals, suicide, heroin, and trains are just a few examples.

Much like virtually everything else that white people like, these notebooks are considerably more expensive yet provide no additional functionality over regular notebooks that cost a dollar. Thankfully, since white people only keep their most original and creative ideas in the Moleskine, many of them will only be required to purchase one per lifetime.

But the growing popularity of these little journals is not without its own set of problems. One of the strangest side effects has been the puzzling situation whereby a white person will sit in an independent coffeeshop with a Moleskine notebook resting on top of an Apple laptop. You might wonder why they need so many devices to write down thoughts. Well, if a white person has a great idea, they write it by hand. If they merely have a good idea, it goes into the computer.

Not only does this help them keep their thoughts organized, but it serves as a signal to the other white people in the shop that the owner of both instruments is truly creative. It screams: "I'm not using my computer to check email and read celebrity gossip, I'm using it to create art. Please ask me about it."

So when you see a white person with one of these notebooks, you should always ask them about what sort of projects they are working on in their free time. But you should never ask to actually see the notebook lest you ask the question "How are you going to make a novel out of five phone numbers and a grocery list?"

12 Messenger Bags

Bicycle messengers are for some reason among the most respected people in the white community. It is unknown if this is due to a particular love of danger, the ability to wear shorts and tights at the same time, or a dedication to delivering packages that makes them so enviable. Whatever the reason, white people love them and try to emulate them as much as possible.

The first trend to emerge out of this fascination was the rise in fixed-gear bicycles. Often ridden by messengers because of their low maintenance and simplicity, they were quickly adopted by white people around the globe. But not every white person wants a bicycle. There had to be another, less dangerous way to get in on this trend. Thankfully, there was the messenger bag.

Wearing one of these bags is a bold statement that you might ride a bicycle and that you like to carry things diagonally. Additionally, the type of messenger bag you wear says a lot about you. Generally the most popular brands are

Timbuk2 and Chrome. Wearing these will get a reasonable level of acceptance, but to go to the next level you need to purchase a bag that is made entirely out of recycled materials.

For some reason, the coolest white people have bags that click together with seat-belt buckles.

You would think that these bags would make for an easy pickup line with white males: "Do you have a package for me?" But that is most likely to make them very uncomfortable as they will have to admit that they are not a real bike courier.

Instead, the best thing you can do with a white person and a messenger bag is to try to get them to play a type of urban midway game called Guess What's in This Bag. To play, all you need to do is find a white person with a messenger bag and at least $10. Simply propose that if you can tell them the contents of their bag without looking, you will get that $10; if you fail to guess the contents, you will tell them about an off-menu item at a nearby ethnic restaurant. When they agree, simply close your eyes, hold your forehead like you are concentrating, and say the following: "Mac laptop, Moleskine notebook, some sort of sandwich, and a book."

And if you are a bag designer looking for ways to improve the messenger bag for white people, simply craft one as it is now but make a pocket for a Pabst Tall Boy and a specialized hummus cooler pocket.

13 Punk Rock

When you get far along enough in your friendship with white people, they are probably going to ask some questions about your life and your tastes in music. Regardless of which angle you are playing with white people (world music, hip-hop, jazz), it's always a good idea to familiarize yourself with punk rock.

It is confirmed that all white people believe that punk music from 1977 to 1980 was important. Though this era only lasted three years, white people have been trying to reenact it during their teenage years for almost three decades.

All white people have had at least a brief period in their life when they  wore Doc Martens boots and only listened to punk music. Or at the very least, they annoyed their parents by playing a Sex Pistols album really loud.

What makes the punk phase so interesting is that white people never have any shame about looking back on it. While they look back with regret at virtually every clothing choice and haircut from ages fourteen to twenty-two, they always look back on their punk phase with fondness. In fact, white people will often remind others about this phase by making their children wear a CBGB or Ramones T-shirt to soccer practice.

Once again you are encouraged to completely suppress the natural urge to point out the inherent hypocrisy in a white person purchasing a kid's size punk rock T-shirt at a high-end children's clothing store to show off that they are a rock-and-roll parent. It would be so easy to just say, "Remember that Buzzcocks song about how difficult it is to buy art big enough to go behind the sofa?" To which they will respond, "No," and you can come back with a satisfying "Exactly." Fight the urge! There is nothing to be gained. Except for maybe impressing slightly younger white people.

14 | Raw Milk

For some reason, white people almost always believe that life was better 150 years ago. Life was simpler, there was less pollution, we ate a more natural diet, and we weren't distracted by all this technology. Of course, they tend to overlook things like racism, disease, poverty, and grueling labor conditions. But then again, these things have long overlooked white people, so it sort of makes sense. Therefore it should come as no surprise that white people have jumped all over the trend of drinking raw milk, or milk that comes directly from the udder of a cow.

Around 150 years ago, we all drank milk this way and as a result we had thriving communities of people with diphtheria and typhoid fever. Then Louis Pasteur came along and fixed the whole thing with pasteurization and those diseases were greatly reduced. But if we've learned one thing from white people, it's that the prospect of a life-threatening disease should not stand in the way of something that is potentially delicious. Even the fact that this is an illegal way to consume milk has not stopped white people from forming small underground collectives where they work under the shadow of night to get their fix of raw milk directly from the farm. As a result, the only way to tell the difference between a group of heroin addicts waiting for their fix and a group of raw milk devotees is the presence of a stroller and a slightly better-condition North Face jacket.

It may seem hard to understand why a group of white people would put this much energy into re-creating a problem that was solved 150 years ago, but remember, these are the same people who reenact the Civil War and listen to vinyl records. Making life needlessly difficult is one of the more enjoyable ways for a white person to fill their massive amounts of free time.

Additionally, dying from drinking a bad batch of raw milk is considered to be one of the most noble deaths in white culture, right up there with bear attack and accidental death during a Greenpeace protest.

So before you accept any social invitation that might cause you to eat breakfast at the home of a white person, you should always ask if they are a part of the raw milk movement. Otherwise that bowl of Kashi cereal could be your last.

Washington, D.C.

- **Overview** Though technically only half white, Barack Obama is America's first truly white president. Jimmy Carter came close, but he expected people to make real sacrifices and white people aren't really into that. No, Obama is the first white president for the following reasons: he went to law school, he attended an Ivy League school, he drives a hybrid, he planted an organic garden at the White House, and he has the one accessory that all white people long for: black children.

- **Strengths** Leader of free world; good jump shot; looks good on a poster.

- **Weaknesses** Cares too much; cigarettes.

- **Secret Shame** In 2003, enjoyed a song by Toby Keith.

15 Promising to Learn a New Language

Historically, white people have a poor record when it comes to promises (see Americans, Native, for examples). Thankfully, modern white people are trying to erase the shame of their past by making new promises to themselves that they will never keep.

Writing a novel, going vegan, or sending their future kid to public school are just a few of these great breakable promises. But by far the most common self-improvement promise is to learn a new language.

This plan is first formulated when white people realize that two years of college Italian does not confer fluency. For the most part, these classes will only teach a white person how to order food in a restaurant, ask for a train schedule, and attempt to correct Italian words that have been adopted into English. ("I think you mean *panino. Panini* is plural.") However, this small amount of proficiency is more than enough for white people to warrant inclusion on their résumé under "Spoken languages."

For many white people the lack of a second language is their greatest secret shame. It fills them with so much shame that they will literally spend the rest of their lives promising to learn a new language, but not so much shame that they will actually do it. When it comes to learning a new language, white people can follow a few paths, the most common of which is to try to learn a language that is spoken widely in their current city. For example, white people in places like Los Angeles or Austin, Texas, will often promise to learn Spanish in hopes of being able to ask local taco stands about whether their carne asada is grass fed (*"¿Ha leído usted Michael Pollan?"*).

In order to reach this level of full fluency (and obnoxiousness), white people believe they must put themselves into full immersion. This means a promise to watch only Spanish-language TV, listen only to Spanish-language radio, read García Márquez in his native tongue, and watch Spanish-language films with the subtitles turned off. There are some instances of white people doing this for almost an entire week!

When this technique is unavailable (or fails), white people will immediately turn to books and computer software as a last-ditch effort to make good on their promise. After about a week, most white people will give up and blame someone for their failure ("This software is terrible," "There aren't enough people in Portland who speak Farsi!"). Rather than discarding the books and software packaging, white people will simply place them in the most visible part of their bookshelf. This allows them to believe that they have not failed, since they can resume their studies but just don't have the time right now.

Because learning a new language is something that most white people fail at, it should be approached with extreme caution. When you hear a white person say that they speak your native language, you will probably think it's a good idea to start talking to them in said language. *Wrong!* Instead you should say something like "You speak [insert language]?" to which they will reply "A little" in your native tongue. If you just leave it here, the white person will feel fantastic for the rest of the day. If you push it any further or speak quickly, the white person will just look at you with a blank stare. Within a minute you will notice that that blank stare has shifted from confusion to contempt. You have shamed them, and your chance for friendship is ruined forever.

Finally, and though they won't admit it, white people do not believe that learning English is difficult. If it were, then that would mean that their housekeeper, gardener, or mother-in-law (if they are an elite white person) is smarter than them. And that realization would have the potential to destroy their entire universe.

The best technique is to just tell white people what they really want to hear: "You should move to [insert country] so you can really learn the language." They will agree instantly and lament their employer's lack of an office there. Share in this lament and you can enjoy a gigantic increase in trust and friendship from that white person.

16 Political Prisoners

If you want to befriend a large number of white people simultaneously, the easiest way to do it is to go to jail for political reasons.

White people love political prisoners because they are individuals who have been locked up due to their beliefs or because their presence stands in defiance of an unjust system. In fact, most white people would love to be locked up for their own beliefs provided that they could go to a jail with private toilets, plenty of books, and no rape.

Since most white people will not end up as actual political prisoners, their best bet is to attend a protest or a benefit concert for a political prisoner. If they are lucky the cops will show up and maybe they will get to go to jail for an afternoon. For white people, being arrested for disorderly conduct at a political rally and then spending an afternoon in jail is known as "police brutality."

If you happen to be a political prisoner, then you have no further work to do. White people already like you and will provide for you financially in the form of book deals, commencement addresses, and documentaries. But even if you are not a political prisoner yourself, you can still benefit.

If a white person asks you to name a personal hero, it is always a good idea to mention a political prisoner. If a white person in the conversation drops an answer like "Kurt Cobain" or "Toni Morrison," you can easily trump them by offering up a name like Mumia Abu-Jamal or Nelson Mandela, which will show white people that you are smart, well informed, and political. Or that you own at least one Rage Against the Machine CD.

But what if you pick the wrong political prisoner? Impossible. This is because political prisoners do not exist until a famous white person has drawn attention to them. Until that point, any person who has been locked up for their beliefs is just a regular prisoner and subsequently not worthy of graffiti stencils.

Conversely, if you ever find yourself needing to end a friendship with a white person, you can simply say something like "Well, he's a criminal, he belongs in jail. I don't care what the Beastie Boys have to say about it." End of friendship.

17 Disinfectant

White people have a number of significant fears: global warming, not leaving behind an artistic legacy, getting fat, the suburbs, and flyover states. But right near the top is germs. All white people live in constant fear of getting a cold since that will prevent them from going outside and performing outdoor activities. There is also a small but vocal group of white people who still believe their children could catch autism from a toilet seat.

This fear has not gone unnoticed by the cleaning supply and personal care product industries. They have been quick to to step in to provide hand sanitizers, grocery cart handle wipes, and antibacterial everything. All of which help to prevent white people, and especially white parents, from having a complete nervous breakdown every single day.

To fully understand the process of how to drive a white person insane, all you really need to do is plant a seed of disgust in their mind. For example: Watch a white person touch a doorknob and then eat an apple or a rice cake. Wait a few seconds, then go up to them and say, "You touched that doorknob. Think about all the people who touched it and what they did before they touched it. Then you touched that food and ate it. I don't want to freak you out, but you should probably make a doctor's appointment. I think you have hepatitis now. Seriously."

Stand back and watch. That white person will immediately begin an elaborate fantasy about the type of people and potential body parts that have come in contact with that doorknob. Once they have settled on something appropriately disgusting, they will visualize the actual touch so vividly and graphically that it will make them dry heave uncontrollably.

Here is where you have two options. If your intended goal was to drive them crazy, simply say, "What else did you touch today?" and walk away. If your goal was to put this white person in your debt, simply step in and hand them some hand sanitizer and a small amount of ipecac. Once the white person returns from the bathroom, they will assume that you have saved their life and will feel they owe you a favor, big-time.

18 | **Taxes**

Though white people are always filled with guilt, there are a few effective ways to alleviate it. Popular techniques involve: running distances for charity, donating money via text message, feeling sad for an appropriate amount of time, and giving spare change to the homeless. But none of these is as effective and more satisfying than paying taxes.

When white people think about high taxes they are reminded of many of their favorite things: Europe, Franklin Roosevelt, free healthcare, and sticking it to people who are richer than them.

The system is perfect for white people because it allows them to feel as though they are attacking the upper classes but doesn't make them give up their car, stand mixer, or *fleur de sel.*

A typical white person's enthusiasm for paying taxes operates on a fairly uniform scale. It begins right in the middle during high school, when white people read their first book by Michael Moore or Howard Zinn. It reaches its apex in college, when they begin reading Marx and the Frankfurt School. During this time white people will be at their most

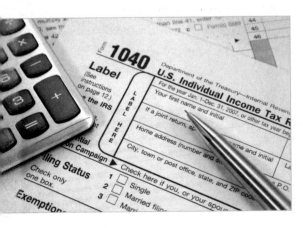

fervent about the need to redistribute wealth among all the classes. Amazingly, this zeal wears off at the exact moment when white people receive their first real paycheck. This love of taxes may abate on a personal level, but in public they can never complain about taxes being too high, for fear of looking like the wrong kind of white person. Instead they must accept their tax burden and ask for more, like Oliver Twist asking for more gruel.

Of course, some white people will spend their entire lives fighting for more taxes to help support education and the arts. They are known in the white community as artists and graduate students. In the rest of the world they are known as "poor by choice." Since neither group is likely to ever make an annual income that requires them to pay taxes, they remain steadfast in their support of increasing taxes for the wealthy, though their very existence is in a way a type of tax upon a very specific group of rich white people called their parents.

Taxes also provide a wonderful way to help you improve the spirits of white people. When tax returns are due and white people are acting stressed-out, you can make white people feel great by saying, "You know, if it weren't for government programs I never would have gone to college. Probably never would have eaten breakfast." Pause, touch them gently on the shoulder, and whisper, "Thanks."

Then ask them if they can spare a few dollars for lunch.

Ideal TV Lineup for White People

Curb Your Enthusiasm
Seinfeld
A documentary
The Rachel Maddow Show
LOST
Battlestar Galactica
Treme
World Cup quarterfinal
Ken Burns's *National Parks*
Twin Peaks
Frontline

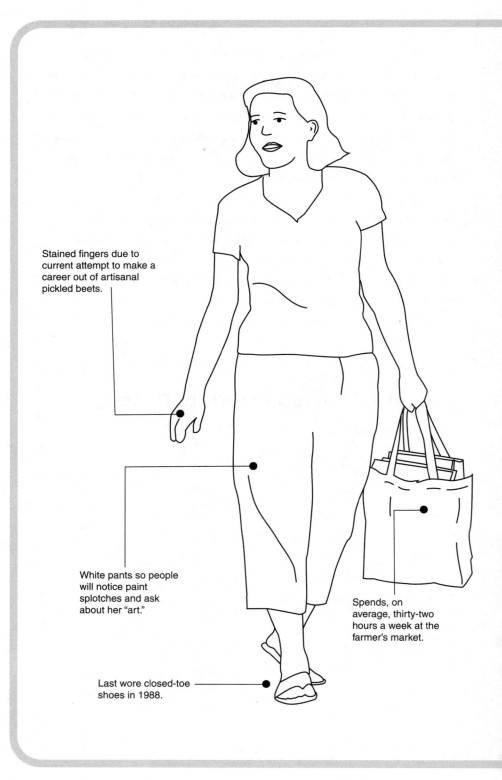

Stained fingers due to current attempt to make a career out of artisanal pickled beets.

White pants so people will notice paint splotches and ask about her "art."

Spends, on average, thirty-two hours a week at the farmer's market.

Last wore closed-toe shoes in 1988.

Asheville, North Carolina

- **Overview** A newer addition to the official list of places white people like to live, Asheville has done an excellent job of providing white people with everything they need to thrive: a large selection of vegetarian restaurants, numerous liberal arts colleges, outdoor festivals, disc golf, and of course, kayaks. With all of these perks, and no real local economy to support a working class, white people are able to live here without guilt and the unpleasant problem of having to look at poor people.

- **Strengths** Good pottery skills; can play an obscure instrument.

- **Weaknesses** Lack of protein has led to muscle atrophy.

- **Secret Shame** Doesn't like "roots" music.

19 | Bumper Stickers

It is a fact that white people will never turn down an opportunity to enlighten other people on the correct way to think. While this is very easy to do through email or face-to-face conversation, it is exceptionally difficult to do while driving a car. Fortunately for white people, there is a solution that is both popular and ineffective: bumper stickers.

Before talking about the types of bumper stickers that white people like, it's very important to get an understanding about layout and placement. When a white person drives an older car (six-plus years old) that has a resale value under $2,000, they will coat the entire backside of the car in bumper stickers. Because of the abundance of space, they are free to include stickers from all areas of white support: music, politics, the environment, insults to right-wing politicians, and various movements imploring people to keep a city "weird."

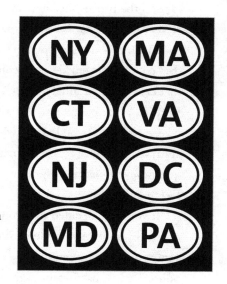

But when white people have a nice new car, such as a Prius or an Audi station wagon, the fear of losing resale value prevents them from applying more than one sticker. Therefore that one sticker must properly capture the essence of the car and the political views of the driver.

The safest and most accepted choice for a sticker is always one that supports a Democratic presidential candidate (Ralph Nader is an acceptable substitute). As of February 2008, white law required an OBAMA '08 bumper sticker to be placed on the back of every Prius. Though these stickers reach peak effectiveness during an election year, it is acceptable to leave this sticker on the car until the next election regardless of whether the candidate actually won. If it's a disputed election, as in 2000, the sticker can be left on for the life of the car.

If a white person does not feel like supporting a candidate, they will likely select a bumper sticker that tells other people what to do. Some popular ones include telling people to COEXIST and to STOP EATING MEAT.

Though there is no conclusive evidence about the effectiveness of these stickers, white people show no signs of abandoning the campaign. In fact, there is a white myth that tells of an unenlightened man who was driving on the freeway and saw a bumper sticker on the back of a Subaru station wagon that read GO VEG. The sticker was so moving that he threw the hamburger he was eating right out the window and became a vegetarian on the spot. Two days later, he affixed the same bumper sticker to his car and the process began anew until enough people had changed their views to form what is now known as the city of Portland, Oregon.

The only other acceptable sticker option for white people is the white oval country tag sticker used commonly in Europe to help identify cars that cross international borders. Though they actually serve a function in Europe, white people use the stickers to show people where they like to take vacations. If you know a white person with one of these stickers, it's always a good idea to ask them about where they got the sticker. Your question will justify the presence of the sticker and make the white person feel great.

If you have decided that you want to improve your status with white people by applying a bumper sticker to your own car, do not make the assumption that you can just use anything! Stickers that support right-wing politics, guns, patriotism, war, or hunting are all unacceptable. It is also unacceptable to use a sticker with a clever slogan that does not support a left-wing political cause. Any of these stickers will likely end any chance you have of befriending a white person.

Note: Attaching a yellow magnetic ribbon to the back of your car will result in your being shunned from some of the stricter white communities and should be avoided at all costs.

20 | Berry Picking

It is well established that white people like the past. Vintage clothing, history degrees, and nostalgia are just three examples of how white people show their love for bygone eras. So when white people think about growing their own food they are reminded of pastoral images of farming, working the land, and growing whole natural foods for their family. This most positive viewpoint comes from the fact that white people have mostly enjoyed supervisory roles in agricultural production over the years.

But as more and more white people moved into cities, they lost their connection to working the land. In recent years the most advanced white people have quit their jobs, moved to the country, and opened artisanal dairies and small-scale radicchio farms.

However, not all white people have the ability, or the trust funds, to quit their jobs, and follow their food-based passions. Some white people have to get their fix by picking their own fruit.

Many of you might be familiar with the process of harvesting a crop. Some of its more intense variations are often referred to as "migrant labor" and "slavery." Under these conditions, laborers are expected to work extremely hard in order to live up to large expectations about their fruit-picking output.

When white people harvest a crop it's known as "berry picking" or "pick your own fruit." Under these conditions, white people are expected to work leisurely with no real expectations and then pay for the privilege to do so. In other words, berry picking is the agricultural equivalent to a private liberal arts college. It's no surprise white people like it, because much like a liberal arts degree it feels like you've done real work when you really haven't.

Of course, the easiest way to turn a profit with this information would be to start your own fruit-picking farm. But that is only looking at the small picture. It is well established that all white people enjoy doing manual labor under watered-down and expensive conditions. So, if you are currently working in a job that requires intensive amounts of work, you should consider using that workspace to create what is essentially an adult day care for white people who would like to spend an afternoon learning how to use a loom or pretending to be a construction worker.

Note: If you encounter a white person who is actually good at manual labor they are either some kind of performance artist, an aspiring writer, or the host of a show on HGTV.

21 The World Cup

Every four years the entire globe comes together to celebrate the World Cup, and since white people make up a pretty significant portion of the world, they are not immune to the excitement.

However, before you start planning out long viewing sessions with white people you should be aware of exactly why they get so excited about the World Cup. While you may be waiting with bated breath for your favorite sport on a global scale, white people like the World Cup because it is a once-every-four-years opportunity to pretend to be European for a few weeks and, more important, to get drunk at odd hours.

Virtually every white person you speak to about the World Cup is incapable of remembering any actual event that took place during a game but can, with near total recall, remember how they got very drunk on sangria during a Spain-Paraguay match at five in the morning.

The sharper readers among you have likely noticed that clever white people also adore the World Cup because it allows them to pair countries with their respective alcoholic drinks.

"England is playing Argentina? Dude we gotta get some Newcastle then and like, I don't know, like some wine I guess?"

This plan will be consummated with a high-five, a trip to Trader Joe's, and the purchase of a soccer jersey that will be worn, on average, twice a decade.

It is also fascinating to note the amaz-ing interest shown by white women in the World Cup. While they generally find most professional sporting events to be boring, the atmosphere at a World Cup match is much more amenable, mostly because they don't have to drink light beer and there is a good chance that they might meet a European man, or at least someone who might be planning a trip to Eu-rope. This is far superior to a hockey game, where at best they might meet a Canadian. So it goes without saying that for white women, the World Cup can't come soon enough.

While hosting a themed party around one of the games is a surefire way to increase your popularity with white people, at the end of the day it will not increase your bottom line. No, during the World Cup, the most profit to be made will come from betting on the games with white people. Not only will they have disposable income, but they will adhere to the following betting patterns:

England is good.
Brazil is good.
Italy is good.
Teams from Africa are cute underdogs and thus always worth a bet.

It goes without saying that you should probably avoid trying to talk to white people about any of the actual players in the World Cup aside from

the biggest stars. Most white people cobble their soccer knowledge together from U.K. celebrity gossip and a few games of FIFA on the Wii.

But if you do find yourself talking to a white person who actually
knows a lot about soccer, you are probably talking to a European or,
worse, a white guy who tries too hard. The latter is especially dangerous,
as they have likely been waiting for years to meet someone to converse
with about "football" (or worse, *fútbol*) and with soccer's year-round
schedule, they will never leave you alone.

22 | Community-Supported Agriculture

We have already examined the complicated relationship
that white people have with food. On one hand they are desperate to participate in the agricultural process (attempting to grow their own food,
paying to do manual labor), but on the other they also don't want to actually have to do anything that requires hard work or leaving their immediate neighborhood.

Looking into this problem, a very intelligent person came up with the
idea of community-supported agriculture, or CSA. Under this policy, a
group of white people pays money to a specific farmer in exchange for direct delivery of fruits and vegetables immediately upon harvest.

This ensures that the farmer will have a market for his harvest and
that white people will get a fresh box of vegetables delivered every week.

This system allows white people to begin a relationship with their
food, something they have been meaning to do since Michael Pollan told
them to do it. But more important, this system gives them an entirely
new way to let vegetables rot in their fridge. Each new box is an opportunity to make a promise and then never cook a recipe that includes ramps,
kohlrabi, or Swiss chard.

During the growing season, white people can also make a visit to one
of these farms. This is considered to be the greatest benefit derived from

joining a CSA: fresh vegetables, being outside, walking around, and being able to say, "I can't believe there are people out there who would rather shop at a supermarket."

It's pretty much a perfect day for white people.

It is not recommended that you ever ask white people to explain this system to you. They will tell you that it's a group of like-minded individuals (white) who band together to support a farmer. They are then investing in the crop, essentially sharing in the crop. To which you will have to resist the urge to say, "So . . . sharecropping. From what I've heard you people usually do pretty well under that system."

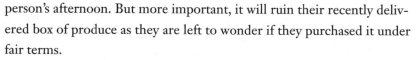

This will ruin both your invitation to the farm and the white person's afternoon. But more important, it will ruin their recently delivered box of produce as they are left to wonder if they purchased it under fair terms.

Then again, if you play your cards right, maybe you can get a free box of peaches.

23 | Duke Basketball

Though many white people will profess to hate Duke basketball and refer to it as the "Cobra Kai" of collegiate sports, there are a number of reasons why deep down, all white people cheer for Duke basketball.

For one thing, most Duke teams are made up of seniors. These players have spent the past four (or five) years of their collegiate lives devoting themselves to basketball—something that they love but ultimately have very little chance of doing professionally and so they will probably have to take a high-paying but soul-sucking job when it's all over. It is the athletic equivalent of an art history degree.

Also, when white people see players so talented that they can leave college early to make obscene amounts of money, it is very upsetting since it reminds them that they are not one of those people. For some reason, they like to believe that their success is based upon a close reading

of Faulkner and not their ambition or entrepreneurial spirit.

But not everyone in Duke basketball is white. They are a diverse team and this is part of their appeal. Though white people cannot admit it, a black Duke basketball player is pretty much their ideal black friend: smart, athletic, and not scary.

Eats a steady diet of tempeh, cigarettes, and ironic detachment.

In addition to vintage hat also owns a hilariously out-of-date basketball jersey.

Totally knows a guy who works for Adult Swim.

Can talk for six hours about Nike Dunks.

Atlanta, Georgia

- **Overview** White people are drawn to Atlanta for its opportunity. Specifically the opportunity to acquire more than one black friend. Though this is achieved by only the most advanced of white people in Atlanta, that hasn't stopped them from moving into the city and creating a vibrant white community center, or as most people refer to it, Little Five Points.

- **Strengths** Might know a black guy.

- **Weaknesses** Takes jokes about the South personally.

- **Secret Shame** Republican family.

24 | Self-Aware Hip-Hop References

Among the wrong kind of white people, few are more hated than the wigger or whitethug. Though it is very acceptable and common for the right kind of white people to dress and act as though they are Japanese, Chinese, or European, it is completely unacceptable for them to act like rappers.

This distaste caused a dilemma for white people, who had to show not only that they loved hip-hop but also that they were aware of their whiteness. The brilliant solution they came up with was to co-opt hip-hop words and mannerisms and filter them through a white-appropriateness system.

For example, white people find it particularly hilarious to take slang and enunciate every word perfectly.

"Homey, that béarnaise sauce you made is wack. Do you know what I am saying? For real."

"Well, I used a different type of butter. I switched the style up, so let the haters hate and I'll watch the deliciousness pile up."

Since the above exchange involves people who are very aware of their whiteness, it is hilarious, but if it were to be said by wiggers, it would be tragic. The difference is subtle but essential.

This is also an excellent way to make white people like you. If you can recite rap lyrics with perfect enunciation, they will always find it funny. As a rule of thumb, the more popular the rapper, the funnier it gets. Best options: 50 Cent, Tupac, Biggie Smalls, or Jay-Z. Note: Avoid Kanye West, as the irony of reciting his lyrics with perfect English is not as great.

In terms of physical actions, there are few things white people enjoy more than throwing up fake gang signs in photos. Again, the same rules apply: if it's done by wiggers it is tragic, but if it's done by the right kind of white people, it is hilarious. It's not a good idea to mention how these signs have often resulted in awful, senseless deaths—that will ruin the joke.

In both cases, the actions are done in hopes that a white person will be recognized as "one of the good ones," who love hip-hop but don't try to appropriate it in any nonhilarious ways.

In both cases, your best response is to say, "Did you go to the last Dead Prez/Roots/Mos Def/Talib Kweli/K'Naan/Michael Franti concert? It was incredible. I smoked weed and kept this one finger up for almost an hour!"

Though this information has very little use in and of itself, it could be the final piece in the puzzle of cementing your white friendship. At the very least, it is a guaranteed way to help your progress.

25 Trivia

Though they are loath to actually say it, all white people consider themselves to be the smartest in their group of friends. Since they can't actually say it out loud, they are always looking for ways to prove it that don't involve standardized test scores, the prestige of their alma mater, or comparing salaries.

For the most part their opportunity to prove their intelligence comes in small, short bursts of specialized knowledge. For example, correcting another white person at a party on things like the original lineup of the Rolling Stones is great, but at most, two, maybe three people will hear it.

What white people have been searching for is some sort of group environment where they can answer a series of questions to prove exactly how smart they are. Thankfully, they have trivia.

Traditionally this trivia has been delivered in the form of board games. But again, those games can be played with at most eight people. And as white people have learned from graduate-level seminars, proving your intelligence to eight people is a bit like working at a nonprofit organization: feels great until you realize that your efforts were pointless.

That all changed with the creation of bar trivia, which has enabled white people to establish the intelligence hierarchy in their group of friends while also proving the full value of a liberal arts education to a bar filled with people trying to do the exact same thing.

If you're invited to one of these events or just find yourself at a bar where this is taking place, there are a few things you should know. Unlike a traditional competition, where people will brag about their ability and make their intention of winning abundantly clear, white people must pretend that they don't care about the outcome of the contest.

This is entirely because of a white person's need for self-preservation in the event that they don't win. If they do actually manage to win, they will joke to their friends about how lucky they were, while secretly enjoying a giant confidence boost. But if they finish second or third, they will blame the loss on drinking or "getting dumber since they left college" and simply try to laugh it off. But make no mistake: they are crying on the inside.

26 Adult Swim

Adult Swim is a block of programming on the Cartoon Network that has produced such original shows as *Aqua Teen Hunger Force, Squidbillies, Sealab 2021*, and *Space Ghost Coast to Coast*. All of the shows feature irreverent, offbeat humor that is universally enjoyed by white people. Oftentimes younger white people will refer to this type of humor as "random," which is confusing considering it is a completely inaccurate use of the word. But they are young; they will learn.

To fully understand why white people love this channel so much you have to understand the world of "under-

ground animation," which is something that has been beloved by white people since *Fritz the Cat*. The more hard-core white people (single white men) will often take their passion for this type of animation so far as to attend an "Alternative Animation Festival," often held at movie theaters you thought were long abandoned. These events are generally made up of cartoons that show famous cartoon characters having sex or swearing.

If you are looking for a relationship with an unsuccessful white male with few job prospects, these festivals are second only to World Bank protests in terms of sheer numbers of ineffectual men.

But Adult Swim has a broad appeal to white people, and as a rule virtually every white person has at least one season of *Aqua Teen Hunger Force* on their DVD shelf.

While you could use these DVDs to entertain yourself, it is not recommended. Instead you should secure one and watch the whole thing in private to test your progress with white people. If you find it funny, congratulations! You are ready for deep and meaningful friendship with white people. If you do not find it funny, you have some work to do.

27 Whole Wheat

Many cultures deal with the concept of compulsion. That is a higher power compelling you into action almost against your will. In some cultures, this compulsion can drive some to religious ceremony, others to charity, and even others to violence. In white culture, people are compelled by something much more important: whole wheat. It would be nice to believe that a white person has a choice in bread or cereal, but in reality they don't.

When a white person is asked "Whole wheat or white?" they are legally prohibited from saying "white." Watch them at any sandwich shop or restaurant where they are given a choice. It is so ingrained in their

heads that when presented with a list of options they will not let the waiter continue after he has said the words *whole wheat*.

When a white person eats whole wheat bread, it's pretty much as close as they will come to experiencing communion. Except instead of accepting the body of Christ, they are accepting a well-balanced diet and their daily recommended intake of fiber and riboflavin.

To reject whole wheat in favor of white bread is tantamount to rejecting a communion wafer in a Catholic church. Though some might say that rejecting the whole wheat is a far more major crime. At least the Catholic church has absolution.

Though they strongly prefer whole wheat bread, white people will eat white bread when there are no other options. And they will generally enjoy it, making the best of a bad situation.

When this happens you might be tempted to tell white people that being forced to choose white due to a lack of options sounds like your collegiate dating career. It is recommended that you avoid this, as white people might find this offensive. Not because you were forced to date white people, but because it will remind them that they are going to have to get their fiber from something else.

Detroit, Michigan

- **Overview** There is some evidence that white people used to live in Detroit, but it is currently the subject of debate. There are also rumors that white people with no money or simply meager trust funds (referred to in white culture as "artists") are beginning to move into the area. But this remains unconfirmed.

- **Strengths** Survived Detroit.

- **Weaknesses** Real estate equity.

- **Secret Shame** Non-ironic purchase of Insane Clown Posse's *The Great Milenko*.

28 Sea Salt

Regardless of how often a white person cooks or how long they have lived in their current home, they all have a tube of sea salt in their pantry. In fact, it's one of the few foodstuffs that white people will actually bring with them when they move. This is because sea salt is expensive and while white people have money, they didn't get that way by throwing away $7 packages of salt.

When white people think about regular salt, all they can think about is sodium and poor health. When they think about sea salt they think about France. So it's no surprise that it has become so popular.

But sea salt is like Trader Joe's, Banksy, or the Shins—entry level to its field. Therefore it is important that you learn about other, more expensive salts such as pink Himalayan, black Hawaiian, and *sel gris*. This knowledge will allow you to complain about not having them. To a white person, this shows that you know and love expensive things but feel sad that you can't yet afford them.

From here you can fill up an entire evening by making the same complaints about art, real estate, or Europe.

29 | Flea Markets

One of the best things about a farmer's market is that you can get food there. One of the worst things about a farmer's market is that you can *only* get food there. If only there were a way for you to go shopping outside in a dog-friendly environment and you could buy vintage clothes, vinyl records, mid-century modern furniture, and kitchy pop culture items from the 1950s and '60s. Wait, there is! It's called a flea market, and it's tailor-made for white people.

Forget your old visions of flea markets as a place where strange and

poor people shopped for necessities and novelty items. Those days are over. Once again white people have taken over something that poor people used to like and made it extremely expensive. Sort of like what they did to Brooklyn, and Asheville, and Portland, and Silver Lake, and denim.

The popularity of the flea market has grown in recent years as it has found a wonderful niche in a perfect white Saturday. With hours that often fall between 9 A.M. and 3 P.M., the flea market can easily be fit into your time between brunch and dinner. A successful brunch followed by a clothing or furniture score at a flea market is about as close to a perfect day as white people are ever going to get.

Sadly, unless you are sitting on a boatload of old headphones or cigarette advertising, the flea market will be of little financial or social benefit to you in your mission to befriend and understand the white race. However, if you want to play a fun game with white people, tell them you know about a secret flea market just outside the city. You have never been but you have a map and you've heard stories of people scoring mint-condition

Scandinavian credenzas for $150. But be warned: they won't leave you alone until you divulge the location.

Acceptable Reasons for a White Breakup

- **@aol.com, @hotmail.com, or @yahoo.com email address.** If your choice of email service providers reflects upon you, what does it say to have your emails and your grandmother's come from the same place? Religious inspirational forwards are just one step away.

- **Lack of familiarity with Russian authors.** Theoretically you could be at a party and a discussion of Pushkin or Solzhenitsyn could break out. If your mate interjects with "Who is Pushkin?" there is a good chance you will lose most of your friends and potentially your job. Having a spouse with a good grasp of literature is a bit like a bicycle helmet—it's probably not very attractive, but it's great to have in emergencies.

- **Dave Matthews Band CD.** It's bad enough to be seen with a CD collection (how did the rest of 1999 turn out?), but to be seen with the messiah of fraternity boys on every continent is completely unforgivable. This one is so bad that even if it was purchased ironically, there will always be the question "Maybe he's actually into that Crash song . . . OMG what if he wants it to be our wedding song?" That fear alone makes a breakup completely justified.

- **Discovery of *The Da Vinci Code* on shelf.** White people would rather have you look through their medicine cabinet than their bookshelf. You can go to rehab for Vicodin addiction; you can't go to rehab for Dan Brown.

- **Affinity for processed sugars.** This needs no explanation.

- **Ordering a Miller Lite.** If this needs to be explained to you and you are dating a white person, then there is a good chance that someone is on the verge of breaking up with you.

- **Agreeing with something said on Fox News.** Even if it was a weather forecast, this is unacceptable.

Thinking about a journalism degree from Northwestern.

Real hope is for Chicago to get a better art scene.

Cubs fan.

Petrified his son will get a journalism degree from Northwestern.

Owns twenty-six polo shirts.

Selvage jeans.

Summer uniform for white, Midwestern dads.

Chicago, Illinois

- **Overview** Chicago is a city of contrasts when it comes to white people. On one hand you have the prototype for suburban fathers across the country—khaki shorts and bright white New Balance shoes. These white people can be seen all over the United States anywhere that souvenirs are sold. However, it's their children (also pictured) who actually make up the majority of Chicago's burgeoning white population. This new breed of white people is out working hard every day and waiting to be told what to do from their leaders: Jeff Tweedy of Wilco and Ira Glass of *This American Life*.

- **Strengths** Direct line to the White House.

- **Weaknesses** Willing to trade soul for Cubs World Series win.

- **Secret Shame** Prefers pizza from New York City.

30 | Ugly Sweater Parties

Over the course of a calendar year, white people have ample opportunities for themed parties and drinking: Halloween, St. Patrick's Day, and Cinco de Mayo are the most popular officially sanctioned holidays. But that does not mean that white people shy away from creating their own impromptu themed parties—Mustache Party! Nineties Prom! *Designing Women*!

During the month of December, white people face an especially difficult challenge. This is the time of year when parties and drinking are most appropriate, but the most obvious theme (Christmas) must be avoided. Christmas forces Christianity upon others, and though their ancestors had no problem with this activity, modern white people are quite disgusted by the idea. Hanukkah parties are fun, but a bit too exclusive, and a Kwanzaa party requires an enormous amount of physical, mental, and ironic labor that can only be done by the most elite of white people.

White people needed to find a party completely free of religious affiliations but still connected enough to the idea of Christmas that they can serve eggnog and hot toddies. The answer: ugly sweater parties.

These parties feature festive drinks, Christmas music by Sufjan Stevens, and most important, intentionally hideous sweaters. These ugly sweaters provide white people with an invisible shield that protects them from any criticism that might emerge if any Christianity accidentally slips into the evening.

"Hey man, I love that Burl Ives song, but, um, you let 'Silent Night' slip into the party mix. That's kind of awkward because, you know, the Crusades?"

White person points to sweater and makes a funny face.

Order is restored.

If you find yourself invited to one of these parties, you must begin your preparations immediately. Craftier white people have been searching used clothing stores since last Christmas, so you should not expect to find anything of significant ironic value. Your best hope is to see if any of your family members has an old sweater lying around.

"Hey man, nice sweater. It's so ugly."

"Yeah, when my family first got to this country we had to shop at Goodwill. This is the first one my father bought to get him through his first winter here. Good thing they didn't have these parties back then, right? He would have died."

"Geez, man, I'm sorry. You can cut in line for eggnog."

31 | Anthropologie

White people love the discipline of anthropology (see Barack Obama's Mother) as a field of graduate study. In fact, you could probably say that white people love everything about anthropology, so when a store opens that takes the French word for the subject as its name, you can only imagine the reception.

If you are hoping to have any sort of friendship or relationship with a white woman, it is a must that you learn about Anthropologie. You might have walked past it a few times at your local mall and wondered how they crammed the interior of a late-nineteenth-century barn into a shopping center that was built in 2005.

When you step inside, the aged hardwood floor and antique bird-houses and worn furniture will transport you to a time period that never existed but is able to somehow seamlessly merge elements from disparate decades. In other words, Anthropologie is the store equivalent of a Wes Anderson film, which certainly helps to explain its appeal.

Everything they sell at this store is brand-new but looks as though it's come from a thrift shop. So you might be wondering why white people would shop here instead of a much cheaper thrift shop. The answer is that while thrift shops will occasionally contain a gem like a perfectly worn velvet couch from the forties, for the most part they are filled with old computers, exercise equipment, and black pro wrestling T-shirts. White women do not have the time to search through racks and racks of shoulder-padded clothing to find the perfect lace dress that will likely not be in their size.

Anthropologie offers white women a thrift store with all the bad taken out (unfashionable clothes, strange smells, actual poor people) and only the good left behind. As an homage to its inspiration, the store still keeps things buried under tables and in bins that require some digging. This enables a white person to feel as though they have accomplished something by locating a knit top, but it does not prevent them from finding a similar product when they are in a hurry.

If the concept is still difficult to grasp, the simplest way to explain it is that Anthropologie is the most efficient way for white women to look and (hopefully) live like Amélie. If you have not seen *Amélie*, do so at your earliest convenience. It is essential to understanding white people.

When the time comes to provide a white woman with a gift, you can approach it from one of two angles. If she prefers clothing over home décor, you should get her a gift certificate. It will show that you understand her. If she likes home décor, go to the store and buy something like a doorknob or salt shaker. Then tell her that you got it from an estate sale from a delightfully eccentric old woman on your street. For some unknown reason, crazy old women are universally recognized as the best former owners of stuff.

32 Monty Python

White people have loved Monty Python for quite some time now. Considering that Monty Python are British, first appeared on public television, and have gone on to create some of the most popular films in white person history, it is no surprise.

It would be normal to assume that all white people love Monty

Python, but it's simply not true. You see, there is a very large, very specific group of white people who do not find the British comedy troupe to be entertaining. They are called women.

It's not that white women are incapable of finding the humor in Monty Python. Quite the opposite. They have all the skills needed to appreciate the jokes: understanding of absurdist humor, love of all things British, understanding of world history and high culture references. No, what has driven white women away from Monty Python is the fact that every white male they have ever met has peppered them with so many reenactments that it's impossible to see the troupe as anything more than an annoyance.

For decades, white women have been dating men who won't shut up about dead parrots pining for fjords, the Ministry of Silly Walks, and the

Knights Who Say Ni. If you don't get any of these references then you are an excellent candidate to start dating a white man. As a nonwhite woman, you are very appealing to white men, in no small part because dating you would mean that they have at least two years of fresh Monty Python material with which to try to impress you.

33 | Improv

In most normal situations, if you were going to give up your time and money to see someone put on a show, you would hope that the performers would practice, or at the very least prepare something in advance to entertain you. Not white people. For years they have been enamored with a style of humor called improv.

At its core, improv is where a bunch of white people onstage take suggestions from the audience and then make something up. It's a bit like charades but with a cover charge.

The white person's passion for improv begins in high school, where they will join a club of like-minded individuals. If you've ever looked through someone's yearbook and thought, "What's the easiest way to find all the nerds who are bad at math?" simply flip to the improv club's page and you will have your answer.

As these budding improv players reach college, the passion intensifies as they break off into smaller "troupes" with wacky names. As a rule of thumb the best improv names are generally wordplays on historical figures, popular films, people, or television shows. For example the Betty White Stripes, Kirk Cameroon, or the Andrew Jackson Five. It is unknown why white people find this wordplay to be so funny, but if you follow white people on Twitter you've probably already figured this out after a barrage of tweets following someone who wrote #IfBandsWereFood.

After college, white people can find improv in literally every city in America, with the main hubs being Chicago, New York, and Los Angeles. White people simply cannot get enough of it, and white improv performers are willing to give up their time, money, and, for the performers, potentially lucrative careers.

When you arrive at an improv event, you will notice that the crowd is made up almost entirely of only the friends and family of the performers. As you have probably already noticed, guilt is a powerful motivator for white people, and an improv show is proof positive that even white people have figured out how to use white guilt to their advantage.

There are rumors that there are nonwhite people participating in this activity, but judging by the cast of *Saturday Night Live* and every sketch comedy show on television, this would appear to be false.

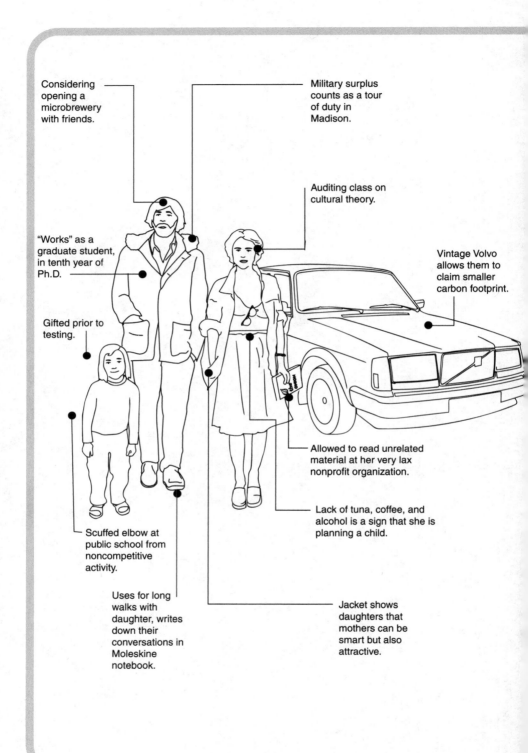

Considering opening a microbrewery with friends.

Military surplus counts as a tour of duty in Madison.

Auditing class on cultural theory.

"Works" as a graduate student, in tenth year of Ph.D.

Vintage Volvo allows them to claim smaller carbon footprint.

Gifted prior to testing.

Allowed to read unrelated material at her very lax nonprofit organization.

Scuffed elbow at public school from noncompetitive activity.

Lack of tuna, coffee, and alcohol is a sign that she is planning a child.

Uses for long walks with daughter, writes down their conversations in Moleskine notebook.

Jacket shows daughters that mothers can be smart but also attractive.

Madison, Wisconsin

- **Overview** With some of the best public schools in America, a venerable NPR affiliate, a major university, and access to the freshest Pabst Blue Ribbon, it's no surprise that white people have been flocking to Madison for generations. Madison is the best place in the world to raise children if you don't have any ambition.

- **Strengths** Resistance to cold; swimming ability; detached sense of humor.

- **Weaknesses** Alcoholism.

- **Secret Shame** Doesn't know who Robert La Follette is and is too embarrassed to ask.

34 | *The Onion*

Before you begin hanging around with white people, you should know that all white humor comes from three sources: *The Simpsons*, Monty Python, and *The Onion*. If you are not presently familiar with *The Onion*, you should visit TheOnion.com immediately, as it is essential in your development and cultivation of white friendships. If you are not familiar with *The Onion*, your conversations with white people will be boring, humorless, and unlikely to lead anywhere productive.

Before moving on, it's important to know exactly what *The Onion* is and where it came from. *The Onion* is a satirical newspaper and website that was founded in Madison, Wisconsin—a very popular location for white people. When the publication got more popular it moved to New York. Since then it has produced a body of work that includes audio, video, and thousands of articles that entertain white people every single day of the year.

It is so popular that every white person's home contains at least one book from *The Onion*. If that home is occupied exclusively by white men, said book will be located in the bathroom. There are no exceptions.

At any given time a white person has 100–200 *Onion* headlines memorized and ready for deployment in a conversation. In fact it is impossible to talk to a white person for more than one hour without hearing

"That reminds me of the *Onion* article. . . ." In order to remain a viable part of the conversation it is essential that you be able to quickly suggest a related, but different, *Onion* article on a similar subject. Doing so will show the white person that you are smart and have a good sense of humor.

As an institution, *The Onion* is beyond reproach for white people. You should not imply that you don't get it or that it's not funny. In fact, the only acceptable criticism for *The Onion* is that you are unable to work for them. This is because every white male under thirty-five is convinced that he could and should be working for *The Onion*.

35 | Vespa Scooters

Within white culture, your choice of transportation method says a lot about you. For example, a Prius says you care about the earth, a bicycle shows you *really* care about the earth, and a bus shows that you are probably not white. But these three options are not the only viable ways for a white person to get around. They have literally dozens of choices, including Volvos, old Mercedes that run on vegetable oil, Subaru Outbacks, and Vespa scooters.

As it stands, every single white person on earth either owns, has owned, or is dreaming about owning a Vespa scooter. And why not? They are Italian, feature vintage design, have low emissions, make the rider look more sophisticated, and carry a little bit of risk. In fact, were it to have a liberal arts degree and a steady income, a Vespa scooter would possess every important quality that a white person looks for in a spouse.

In addition to these superficial qualities, Vespas provide some very practical benefits to white people. Namely, scooters are perfect for gentrified neighborhoods, which are often short on parking and heavy on people who are impressed by Vespas.

If you are in search of a fun game, a white person who has recently purchased a Vespa can be a source of tremendous entertainment. Step

One: Get them talking about their Vespa (easy). Step Two: Start asking them why they didn't save money by getting a Honda or Suzuki that gets the same mileage. Step Three: See how many of the following justifications a white person will use during the ensuing rant: environment, parking, urban lifestyle, union labor, writers, fuel efficiency, *Roman Holiday*, study abroad, and being into Vespas before everyone else.

Finally, the Vespa has produced one of the great paradoxes in white culture. Vintage Vespas are infinitely cooler than newer ones, but the vintage models produce more pollution than most automobiles. If you know a white person facing this dilemma, just say something like "The amount of energy and carbon used to produce a new scooter will probably cancel out the emissions from your vintage one."

Problem unsolved forever.

36 | Short Stories

White people have dreams of being a novelist. Unfortunately, time, talent, and money often get in the way of the opus that will finally spring a white person from obscurity and into well-deserved fame. So what can a white person do when they want to create a book but don't have that much time or energy to spare? They shorten it, distribute it to their friends, and call it a day.

Though this is not a surprising statistic, white people are the sole producers and consumers of short stories in America. It's true!

Of these stories produced by white people, the best will often find their way to *The New Yorker*, where they will be not read by thousands of intelligent white people. If the story isn't good enough to make *The New Yorker*, it will likely end up in a literary journal run by other white people who write short stories.

The typical white person short story can be written by just about anyone. Simply write a story where you spend a lot of time describing the characters, and make sure that nothing happens. If a story has a clear beginning, middle, and end, that means that a white person will understand exactly what you were trying to accomplish in your story. And while you would think that comprehension would be prized, most white people view it as a sign that the story was simplistic and poorly written.

No, to really capture the minds of white people you must write a story that doesn't really go anywhere so that when they are finished reading they will be left with a sense of confusion about what they just read. To a white person, a feeling of confusion is the expected response to all forms of "good" art. (For example, next time you are at an art gallery look at the

faces of the white people there. Though they will never admit it, they all wish that paintings would come with a timer beneath them to let them know that they have appreciated the art for an intelligent amount of time.)

This confusion means it was well done. Additionally, you never have to worry about a white person asking any pesky questions like "So what was that about?" or "Can you explain it to me?" To do so would be to publicly out them as poorly read.

To get an idea about what is an appropriate response to a white person who hands you a short story, you should simply ask them about the Allen Ginsberg poem *Howl*. Take notes, since this is the best example of how to praise something without having read it.

37 Alternative Newspapers

If you live in a reasonable-size city, you have probably seen a newspaper box offering "free papers." These are called alternative newspapers, and they are a vital part of white culture.

Though these papers cover different cities, they are all pretty much identical. The cover will feature either a local story exposing government corruption or a band/rapper you have never heard of. If you can sort through all the advertisements, you will find a number of stories about local restaurants and indie bands, "Life in Hell" cartoons, a Savage Love column, and reviews of movies and books. Prior to the advent of the Internet, this was white people's primary source of cultural information and deals on backpacking vacations to Europe.

By the time you get to the end of the paper, you will likely be struck by the following thoughts: "I didn't know my city had so many futon stores," "How much of this paper is made up of advertisements for prostitution?," "How many drummers does one city need?," and, if you live in California, "Well, I guess I know where to get medical marijuana."

Additionally, the alternative newspaper provides an important step in the career of a white person who wishes to pursue a career in journalism. Currently the path works as follows: college newspaper → alternative newspaper internship → unemployment.

The rare feat of securing an actual full-time (not freelance) job with one of these papers is considered one of the greatest accomplishments in all of white culture. Working as a writer at an alternative newsweekly is one of those high-prestige, low-pay jobs that white people seem to covet so dearly. Other professions in this category include bicycle messenger, graduate student, and bookstore employee.

Thankfully every city with a significant white population has at least one (and in some cases two or three) alternative newspapers. Should you find yourself in a new city looking for local, specific information to help you blend in, there is no quicker route than to simply pick up one of these papers and thumb through it. Not only will it provide you with the information you need to fit in with white people, but your ink-stained thumbs-up will show them that you are to be trusted.

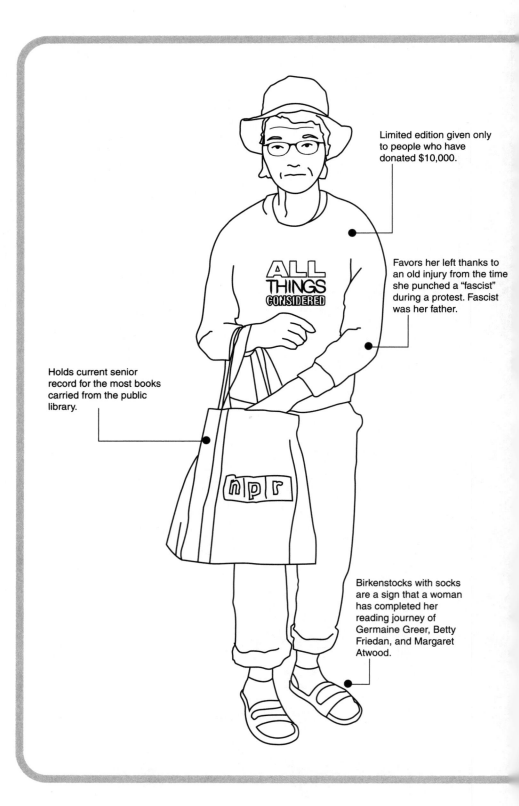

Limited edition given only to people who have donated $10,000.

Favors her left thanks to an old injury from the time she punched a "fascist" during a protest. Fascist was her father.

Holds current senior record for the most books carried from the public library.

ALL THINGS CONSIDERED

npr

Birkenstocks with socks are a sign that a woman has completed her reading journey of Germaine Greer, Betty Friedan, and Margaret Atwood.

Minneapolis, Minnesota

- **Overview** It is a known fact that people from Minneapolis get all of their clothing exclusively from NPR pledge drives. The recent addition of NPR underwear has enabled those in the Twin Cities to finally complete their outfits. Minneapolis is also home to the most disc golf courses in America.

- **Strengths** Excellent lung capacity from cross-country skiing; low rates of obesity.

- **Weaknesses** Cannot say no to Al Franken; easily hypnotized by Prince.

- **Secret Shame** Only cross-country skis out of peer pressure.

38 | Frisbee Sports

Though many white people consider competitive sports to be too aggressive and macho for their tastes, there are a few exceptions. The most notable is soccer. For some reason it is wrong to get fired up about a football game, but right to get fired up about a football match. The second sport (term used loosely) in this category is called Ultimate Frisbee or simply Ultimate.

It is important to know that when you hear a white person saying "We should do some Ultimate this weekend" or "I'm so pumped for Ultimate," they are talking about a sport and not an "ultimate solution" type of race war. Though a quick look at a field full of Ultimate Frisbee players might lead one to surmise that an ethnic cleansing has taken place.

When you first see the sport being played, you will be struck by how amazingly boring it is. Imagine a field of white people running around throwing a Frisbee and trying to catch it in an "end zone." Sometimes one person "guards" another and that's the whole game. There is nothing more to explain.

If you look a little closer, you will uncover some surprising things. First, you will never see hippies get more upset than on an Ultimate Frisbee field. It can be jarring to see people who look like they should be playing acoustic guitars yelling at each other about whether Blake stepped out of bounds. Second, you will notice that Ultimate Frisbee matches are the best place to meet white guys who wear headbands.

Fortunately, Ultimate Frisbee offers a lot of opportunities for personal, professional, and financial gain. Since the sport has yet to be integrated, you could command a high fee in terms of money or favors if you agree to join one of the many white leagues in your area. To a white person, having a diverse Ultimate team is almost as good as winning the championship. Almost.

In addition, white people have also created a sport called disc golf. In this game, you see how many throws it takes to get a disc into a receptacle. There is no other pertinent information about this sport, and its only real value lies in the fact that it is a cheap date for white people who like to be outside.

In any case, if a white person talks to you about a sport that you've never heard of, do not be afraid to ask some questions. This is because, on average, white people invent a new sport every six weeks. Hacky sack, sky surfing, cornhole, and group juggling are just a few of the games invented to help white people maximize their time at parks and beaches.

39 | Camping

If you found yourself trapped in the middle of the woods without electricity, running water, or a car, you would likely describe that situation as a "nightmare" or "a worst-case scenario like after a plane crash or something." White people refer to it as "camping."

When white people begin talking to you about camping they will do their best to tell you that it's very easy and allows them to escape the pressures and troubles of the urban lifestyle for a more natural, simplified, relaxing time. Nothing could be further from the truth.

In theory, camping should be a very inexpensive activity, since you are literally sleeping on the ground. But as with everything in white culture, the more simple it appears the more expensive it actually is.

Camping is a multi-day, multi-step, potentially lethal activity that will cost you a large amount of both time and money. Unless you are in some sort of position where you absolutely need the friendship of a white person, you should avoid camping at all costs.

The first stage of camping always involves a trip to an outdoor equipment store like REI (or in Canada, Mountain Equipment Co-op). These stores are well known for their abundance of white customers and their extensive inventory of things for white people to buy and only use once. If you are ever tricked into going to one of these stores, you can make white people like you by saying things like "Man, this kayak is only twelve hundred dollars. If I use it thirty-five times I've already saved money over renting." Note: Do not actually buy the kayak.

Next, white people will take this new equipment and load it into an SUV or Subaru Outback with a Thule or Yakima roof rack. Then they will drive for an extended period of time to a national park or campground where they will pay an entrance fee and begin their journey. It is worth noting that white people are unaware of the irony of using a gas-burning car to bring them closer to nature, but it is not recommended that you point this out. It will ruin their weekend.

Once in the camp area, white people will walk around for a while, set up a tent, have a horrible night of sleep, and walk around some more. Then get in the car and go home. This, of course, is a best-case scenario. Worst-case scenarios include: getting lost, poisoned, or killed by an animal, and encountering an RV. Of these outcomes, the latter is seen by white people as the worst since it involves an encounter with the wrong kind of white people.

Conversely, any camping trip that ends in death at the hands of nature or requires the use of valuable government resources for a rescue is seen as relatively positive in white culture. This is because both situations might eventually lead to a book deal or documentary film about the experience.

Ultimately the best way to escape a camping trip with white people is to say that you have allergies. Since white people and their children are allergic to almost everything, they will understand and ask no further questions. You should not say something like "Looking at history, the instances of my people encountering white people in the woods have not worked out very well for us."

40 | Losing Weight

There are a number of accomplishments held in high esteem by white people: landing a first internship, running a marathon, seeing a band before they get popular, giving birth to a child without the use of drugs, finishing a Victorian novel. But all of them pale in comparison to the greatest accomplishment in all of white existence: losing weight.

The white person's relationship to obesity is a complicated one. You may have heard white people talking about how much they support overweight ethnic actors that they refer to as "curvy." But the truth is that this support is merely a karmic offering in hopes that whatever spiritual force controls metabolism will shine its light upon them for their acts of kindness to the heavy.

No matter how much a white person will deny it, there is nothing they fear more than getting fat. So it should come as no surprise that losing weight is held in such high regard. It's a physical equivalent to the feeling of a first step in the right direction that white people had when they first moved away from their small hometown or suburb.

Most normal people would lose the weight, accept compliments on their new appearance, and let others continue to live their lives as they see fit. Not white people. When a white person loses weight, it becomes their mission to make everyone around them feel bad for eating or drinking anything that might be responsible for weight gain.

This is not done out of any particular concern for the health or well-being of the people around them, but rather as an attempt to ruin whatever pleasure someone might have gleaned from a bottle of beer or a delicious sandwich.

If you come from a culture that is known for being particularly thin, you can always have some fun with white people by telling them that you can eat whatever you want provided that you drink a certain type of tea afterward. You really don't even need to offer up more of an explanation than "The tea prevents the fat from being absorbed" and they'll believe it! Not only will you have a fun time watching the white person gain weight, but you will clear some outstanding margins on your new tea sales business.

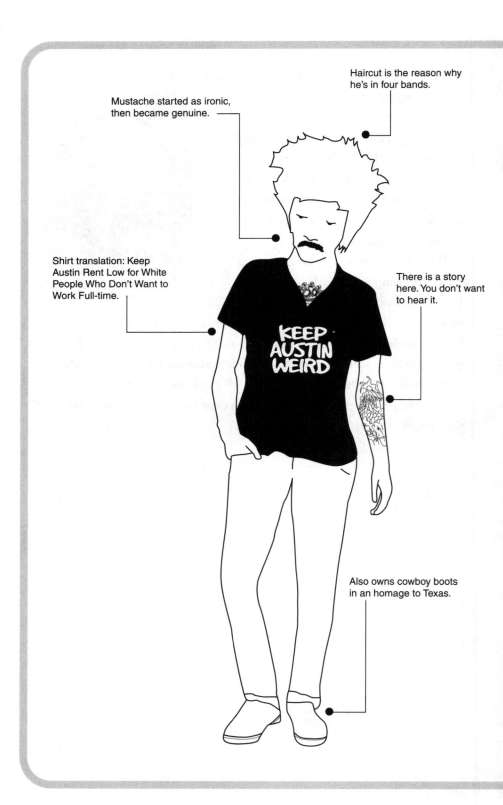

Haircut is the reason why he's in four bands.

Mustache started as ironic, then became genuine.

Shirt translation: Keep Austin Rent Low for White People Who Don't Want to Work Full-time.

There is a story here. You don't want to hear it.

KEEP AUSTIN WEIRD

Also owns cowboy boots in an homage to Texas.

Austin, Texas

- **Overview** It's no surprise that Austin, Texas, is home to many white people. It is the home of Whole Foods, the University of Texas, and Statenfreude. That last term, of course, refers to white people who are simultaneously proud and ashamed of their home state. Though other states have started to experience Statenfreude (notably California, for the first time, after the ban on gay marriage), Austin can lay claim to its origination. The city itself features a wide range of white people, including rich white people and the slightly less rich white people who complain about them. They can be easily found anywhere in Austin that's not Sixth Street on a Friday or Saturday night.

- **Strengths** Able to handle high temperatures; might know Mike Judge.

- **Weaknesses** Legally bound to attend South by Southwest every single year.

- **Secret Shame** Thinks Shiner Bock sucks.

41 | Halloween

When it comes to holidays, there are few that white people like more than Halloween. This is in spite of the fact that white people are required to spend almost the entire year preparing for it. Unlike Thanksgiving or Christmas, the preparation requires little emotional labor, but it does require extensive physical and mental labor along with a fair amount of research.

The Halloween costume is so important to white people because it is a chance to literally show everyone how clever you are without having to say a word. This makes it especially important to single white people, as one well-thought-out costume could produce enough romantic interest to last through the winter.

For this reason any white Halloween party is less of a celebration than it is a contest. And as with any contest, there are rules.

The first thing you need to know is that white people are the only people on the planet who will dress up as a concept. So while your mind considers a costume to be something like "cowboy," "policeman," or "Count Dracula," white people are more likely to think "math," "the economy," or "postmodernism."

Dressing up as a concept is always a major gamble. On one hand, there is the chance that you will nail it just right and everyone in the room will recognize how you not only cleverly interpreted the idea but also executed it perfectly in physical form. If you get it wrong, you will be required to spend the entire night explaining yourself. Either way, it is a good way to get white people to talk to you.

Things do not get any easier if you try to dress up like a character from a movie. If you show up dressed as Austin Powers or Napoleon Dynamite you will be met with near universal scorn. You see, you need to find a character from a movie that enough people recognize but not one who is so well known that it is easy to find the materials required to create the costume.

That being said, it's a good idea to draw inspiration from older movies or television shows, specifically ones from the 1980s. Some popular examples: Pee-wee Herman, the skeleton costumes from Cobra Kai, or Marty McFly. Depending on your race and gender, this could be your opportunity to become the alpha dog among your white friends.

The only thing white people like more than costumes is group costumes. So if you are an Asian male of any background, suggest to your white male friends that you all dress up as the Goonies. If you are a black female, offer to play the role of Tootie and go as the girls from *The Facts of Life*. This is considerably tougher for a black male. But if you are short enough the role of Webster could be right for you, or you could do *Diff'rent Strokes* with an ensemble cast. Sadly, if you do not fall into one of these categories your opportunity for a group costume is limited, since there are no recorded instances of white people befriending Asian women, Latinos, Indians, or any other race during the 1980s. Or at least not instances that white people associate with a fun party.

Last, but certainly not least, are white people who dress up as characters from books that have not been made into well-known movies.

> "I'm Esther Greenwood."
> "Who's that?"
> "Um, from *The Bell Jar*, hello?"
> "I'm sad, too."

These people are unlikely to be recognized as their characters but are highly recognized as being smart. If you cannot pull off a group costume, this is your best bet. Just pick *any* author who shares your heritage, find a character who matches your age and sex, and remember their name. Then show up in regular clothes.

This also allows you to make the awesome joke, "Oh, you can't tell? I'm dressed up as a Sri Lankan woman. Which is what I am." (Substitute race/sex as appropriate.) White people will find this hilarious, unless there is another nonwhite person at the party making the same joke.

You should also be prepared for the guaranteed awkward situation of running into a white person in an offensive costume. It is a certainty that any Halloween party will have at least one white guy dressed up as a recently (and preferably tragically) deceased or wounded celebrity. Past examples include Steve Irwin costumes with a stingray protruding from the chest or Roy (of Siegfried & Roy) with a stuffed tiger attached to the neck.

With this information, you should have no problem fitting right in at a white Halloween party. But don't try too hard at your costume. White people hate being upstaged.

42 | Trader Joe's

With their seemingly never-ending selection of low-priced nuts, energy bars, wine, and appetizers, Trader Joe's has become an essential supply line for white people living in areas not served by a Whole Foods or grocery co-op.

The name of the chain comes from the role it plays in the white person colonization process. When white people decide to take over a once-dilapidated neighborhood, they first send scouts known as "artists," "freelancers," or, as you might know them, "unemployed." Driven with the same level of zeal as early Jesuit missionaries to Quebec, these white people are drawn to the neighborhood by low rents and authentic ethnic experiences. One key difference, however, is that while the missionaries hoped to convert people to Christianity, white people simply hope to convert property.

Eventually the French would set up a trading post where natives could

sell animal pelts in exchange for muskets, cloth, knives, and kettles. A Trader Joe's does almost the exact same thing, except instead of survival goods they stock soy meat products, baby carrots, and turkey bacon.

Another key difference between early trading posts and Trader Joe's is the employees. Whereas the trading posts were staffed mostly by ambitious young entrepreneurs, Trader Joe's seem to be staffed entirely by people who were laid off by independent music stores.

When you are at the checkout counter you might be surprised at how friendly the clerk is and how eager they are to tell you that the prepackaged Jaipur vegetables are delicious with the organic brown rice. Your first instinct will be to look around for a tip jar or some other method that they will use to convert this kindness into money, but there is none. The employees are simply happy to be working at a place that will allow them to stock shelves at a snail's pace while they talk about the recent concert of the cashier on register three.

Ultimately, a Trader Joe's simply signifies that a neighborhood is an acceptable place to live. And while this mostly happens in gentrifying neighborhoods, the power of Trader Joe's is so strong that it can even make suburbs and flyover states acceptable.

"Oh, you guys have Trader Joe's here?"

"Yeah, we've had it for about nine years."

"Hmmm, maybe I could live in Columbus, Ohio, after all."

43 Products Made by People Named Tom

A product named after a single person is very comforting to white people. Burt's Bees and Newman's Own are just two examples of how white people like to believe that they are buying their beauty products and salad dressing from a real person and not a corporation. Of course, in many cases they actually are buying these products from a big corporation, but it's best not to point that out. It could ruin their enjoyment of an eighteen-dollar shampoo.

But of all the names that are popular with white people, nobody seems to make a better product than a man named Tom. The first popular white Tom is the man behind Tom's of Maine, a company that produces a full line of all-natural products that don't work. If you're ever stuck behind a white person on a humid day and the body odor is overwhelming, don't think the white person is a victim of poor grooming. Well, unless they have dreadlocks—then, yes, they are guilty of poor grooming. But more likely they have just made the false assumption that an all-natural deodorant and antiperspirant will work. Or even worse, they've been tricked into thinking that a crystal will somehow stop them from smelling when they sweat. Yes, you did read that correctly: virtually every white person has tried and regretted using a deodorant made out of a crystal. This is not a joke.

The other famous Tom for white people is the one who created TOMS Shoes. These canvas shoes are all natural and are sold in Whole Foods. Every time you buy a pair of shoes they donate a pair to a child in need in the third world. Of course, instead of buying a pair of shoes a white person could just donate the money they were going to use on shoes to the TOMS charity and let *two* people in the third world get new shoes. But that's not a realistic possibility, not with summer right around the corner.

If you ever want to completely blow the mind of a white person who owns an old pair of TOMS, simply follow these directions. Step one: Purchase a pair for yourself, the rattier-looking the better. Step two: Ask the white person where they got their shoes. It is a known fact that it is impossible for white people to not tell you the charitable story behind their purchases. When they get to the part of the story where they say that TOMS gives a pair to a child in the third world, simply lift up your pant legs to reveal your shoes and say, "I know . . . thank you, Jacob."

> **WARNING:** The white person will try to hug you after this.

44 | Roller Derby

If you meet a white girl with black hair, tattoos, and a passion for horror films, there is a 100 percent chance that she plays in some sort of Roller Derby league. The sport reached its height of popularity in the seventies, thus all but guaranteeing that white

people would eventually resurrect it in a fit of nostalgia and irony. But the sport draws in white people for many other reasons, including funny costumes and the opportunity for women to compete under clever pseudonyms like Arianna Puffington and Sarah Nailin'.

Once a league forms, schedules are made, websites are put up, venues are booked, and tickets are sold. In all, it's a testament to the incredible work ethic that white people have when it comes to a whimsical activity.

Should you choose to attend an event, you will be shocked at the sheer volume of mustaches and black rock-and-roll T-shirts, and the complete lack of anyone with a full-time job. When the activities start, the women will start skating around in a circle. There are rules and points and strategies, but at most Roller Derby matches the only people who seem to be aware of them are the people playing.

If you know someone who plays on a Roller Derby team, you should treat them like a white person who does improv. Encourage them in their efforts, but make it clear that you will not pay money to watch their hobby.

Stuff White People Think *You* Like

African Americans

1. Soul food
2. African art
3. Tyler Perry
4. Hip-hop
5. Toni Morrison
6. White people who are marginally familiar with anything on this list
7. Slam poetry
8. Your grandmother
9. Spike Lee
10. The Democratic Party

Asian Americans

1. John Woo
2. White spouses

3. Math
4. Asian food (regardless of ethnicity; e.g., "You're Korean; you must love Chinese food")
5. Margaret Cho
6. White people who ate tripe once at a dim sum place
7. Anyone named Murakami
8. Buddhism
9. Classical music
10. Dance Dance Revolution

Native Americans*

1. Nature
2. Wolves
3. White people apologizing
4. People who are one-sixteenth Native American
5. That Rage Against the Machine video; you know the one
6. Turquoise jewelry
7. Dream catchers
8. Using every part of the animal
9. Lacrosse
10. Stories about Andrew Jackson being a dick

Indian Americans

1. *Slumdog Millionaire*
2. Aziz Ansari
3. That Jay-Z song with Panjabi MC
4. Engineering
5. Vegetarians
6. Cricket
7. Dr. Sanjay Gupta
8. Gandhi
9. White people who are thinking about taking a trip to India
10. Spices

* White people, on average, have met one actual Native American in their lifetime.

Latinos

1. Jesus
2. Mariachi bands
3. White people who took Spanish in high school
4. Immigration reform
5. Che Guevara
6. *Y Tu Mamá También*
7. Soccer
8. Gotan Project
9. *One Hundred Years of Solitude*
10. Buena Vista Social Club

Dyed black to help highlight 1/64 Navajo (according to 23andMe), but does not like to be reminded that 63/64 of her heritage is responsible for the death of the remainder.

Sweater provides spiritual connection to "the land."

Cold after holding protest sign in front of planned development that didn't conform to Sante Fe style.

Planning on participating in Native American dance ceremony later this year.

Santa Fe, New Mexico

- **Overview** Santa Fe is known around the world for having some of the toughest building requirements of any city. Everything must be made in accordance with Santa Fe style. White people who live here usually focus on their spirituality, which is some sort of mix between Buddhism, Native American wisdom, and a strange worship of crystals. Though little is known about this religion, one requirement seems to be the purchase of an inordinate amount of pottery and furniture made from logs.

- **Strengths** Learning Annex courses have taught them to make Native American pottery.

- **Weaknesses** Will try to give you the pottery as a "gift."

- **Secret Shame** Once coveted a non-adobe home.

45 Appearing to Enjoy Classical Music

There are a number of industries that survive solely upon white guilt: Penguin Classics, the SPCA, free-range chicken farms, and the entire rubber bracelet market. Yet all of these pale in comparison to classical music, which has used white guilt to exist for more than a century beyond its relevance.

Though white people do not actually listen to classical music, they like to believe that they are the type of people who would enjoy it. You can witness this firsthand by going to any classical performance at your local symphony, where you will see literally dozens of white couples who have paid upwards of $80 for the right to dress up and sit in a chair for hours reading every word in the program.

After leaving the concert hall, white people will immediately begin telling everyone they know about how much they loved the performance and how they plan to "go more often." This is because white people see little to no value in enjoying classical music without recognition from other white people. This can be seen firsthand by looking at the plaques and bricks around all opera houses: they are covered in white person names.

If a white person starts talking to you about classical music, it's essential that you tread very lightly. This is because white people are all petrified that they will be exposed as someone who has only a moderate understanding of classical music. When a white person encounters another white person who actually enjoys classical music (exceptionally rare), it is often considered to be one of the most traumatic experiences they can go through.

> "Really? Beethoven's Fifth Symphony . . . that's your favorite."
> "Um, no, I mean . . ."
> "You sure it's not Pachelbel's Canon?"
> "Well, ah, I like that, ah, song."
> "[Sigh.] Of course you do."

Even the possibility of this conversation happening is enough to scare white people into attending up to (but no more than) two performances in any given classical season. Therefore it is essential that even if you possess a massive amount of knowledge about classical music, you do not share it with a white person regardless of how much they profess to love it. It's a recipe for disaster and shame.

As a defense mechanism against the possibility of being called out for a lack of familiarity with the early works of Antonin Dvorak, white people have started to list more contemporary composers as their favorites. Of course, the easiest way for them to do this is to choose composers with music that appears in independent films. Knowing these composers is almost a golden ticket to making white people think you are smart, but not *too* smart.

The first, of course, is Philip Glass. Not only does he have one of the best last names a white person can have, he also writes music used in smart documentaries, thus combining two things white people are passionate about in a single artist.

The second, and slightly more obscure, is Erik Satie. A composer at the end of the nineteenth century, Satie has risen to prominence among white people because his music has been sampled by popular musicians and featured in a number of independent films. Dropping this name at a dinner party will show that you are modern and postmodern at the same time. It is also a good idea to tell white people that your tastes in general are "modern and postmodern at the same time." Don't worry, you won't have to explain it.

Note: Under no circumstances should you ever list John Williams or Danny Elfman as your favorite composer.

46 | World Music

For many people, the most difficult part of travel is all the logistics: booking rooms, transfers, figuring out where to eat and what to see. It can be a bit overwhelming. But for white people, the biggest challenges of traveling come not during the trip, but after. For you see, after a white person has returned from a trip abroad, they must then set about on a task more challenging than any journey: they must find ways to get other people to ask them about their trip.

It's not easy. White people will put up photos, wear local clothing from their trip, and do whatever they can to induce someone to ask them about their recent travel. It would be so much easier if they could just bring the subject up themselves, but if a white person attempts to steer a conversation toward their journeys too often, they will seem pretentious. While this is accurate, being thought of as pretentious by people who are already pretentious is pretty awful. It's like a group of very smelly people giving you a stick of deodorant for your birthday.

So to combat this problem, white people have plunged headfirst into world music. If they play it loud enough at work or at a dinner party, people are almost guaranteed to say, "Who is this?" To which the white person can say, "You know, when I was in Bolivia, I really got into this flute music. I got this CD from a group of musicians on the streets of La Paz."

Another benefit that white people can glean from world music is that it gives them a new country to care about politically. Knowing that their world music has a political angle will force white people to do research into what has spurred on this furious bongo solo.

> **WARNING:** If you live near a white person who is into world music, start looking for a new place to live. They are literally days away from buying a new instrument.

47 Photography

Becoming a successful artist often takes years of training and study, something that white people are fully capable of doing. It also requires a degree of ability and talent, which is something that white people are capable of believing that they possess innately, even though that probably isn't true. But that doesn't stop them in their need to be seen as creative. What they need is some sort of system whereby they do not need any actual talent but can still create something that is considered to be artistic.

Photography!

For a photograph to be considered art, a white person need only take a blurry picture of a skyline, blow it up, then mount it to their wall. If they take the same photo with a vintage camera, specifically a Leica, then it is groundbreaking.

This need to create art by simply pushing a button has spawned one of the most popular iPhone applications in history: Hipstamatic. It gives white people all the effect of shooting something with a vintage camera without all the mess of developing film or actually having to own a vintage camera. Now a white person can take a picture of their friend looking out the window of a bus or a train and it doesn't look pretentious. Well, it still looks pretentious but at least it looks vintage pretentious, which is often known in white circles as "the good kind."

In addition to this artistic photography, white people have also started to take pictures of their food before they eat it. Some white people do this as a spiritual tribute to the food they are about to eat, but most white people do it so that they can post to Facebook or Twitter and prove to their friends that they ate from a cool food truck before it became too popular.

Another possible reason why white people over thirty take so many pictures of their food is that once white people cross the thirty-year mark, they replace their passionate knowledge of indie bands with an equally passionate and judgmental attitude toward restaurants. So instead of sharing photos of themselves at a Bon Iver concert, they much prefer to look at plates featuring foie gras.

Regardless of the reason behind the photography, white people will keep doing it till their dying breath. Some will try to get a small amount of Internet fame by taking a picture of themselves or their child every day for a few years, while others will simply continue with food photography. It should be noted that the most advanced of these white photographers will often brag that their Creative Commons–licensed photographs have been featured on a site that ends in -*ist*.

Do not bother asking if they were paid for their photos. The answer is always "No . . . not yet."

48 | Supporting the Troops but Not the War

It's not exactly a secret that white people are strongly antiwar. They have been against all forms of armed conflict since the end of World War II. Since then, just take a look at any antiwar protest and you are virtually guaranteed to see a throng of white people with elaborate and clever signs stating their displeasure with the current government and its war.

For the most part, when white people are discussing war they are speaking to other white people who already agree with them. So rather than having to engage in a debate about the need for armed conflict, they can simply pat themselves on the back for being opposed to the war and then throw out some information about Halliburton or Kellogg Brown & Root. These are known as "serious talks" and when they are finished everyone feels good about themselves and their beliefs.

But from time to time white people find themselves in one of the most awkward situations they will ever face: criticizing the war in front of someone who has a child in the military.

This often comes about when white people make the assumption that everyone around them is exactly the same as them. Additionally, most white people operate under the assumption that the last white person to serve in the military was John Kerry.

Faced with the twin problems of having directly insulted someone's child and potentially being forced to admit they were wrong, white people needed a solution. That solution was to say that they support the troops and not the war.

Technically this is an entirely new insult that implies that the troops are dying for nothing. It provides enough cover for white people to assume that they are still liked by the military person that they just insulted. Whether it's actually true is completely irrelevant.

But before you let your anger build up toward these white people, remember that this really isn't their fault. When white people say they support the troops and not the war, they are actually saying that they support spending time and money training the troops for combat, but that they also support never actually using them in real-life conflict. To you it might seem silly to spend all this energy learning skills that you'll never use, but the truth is that white people have been supporting a system like this for years. It's known as a liberal arts education.

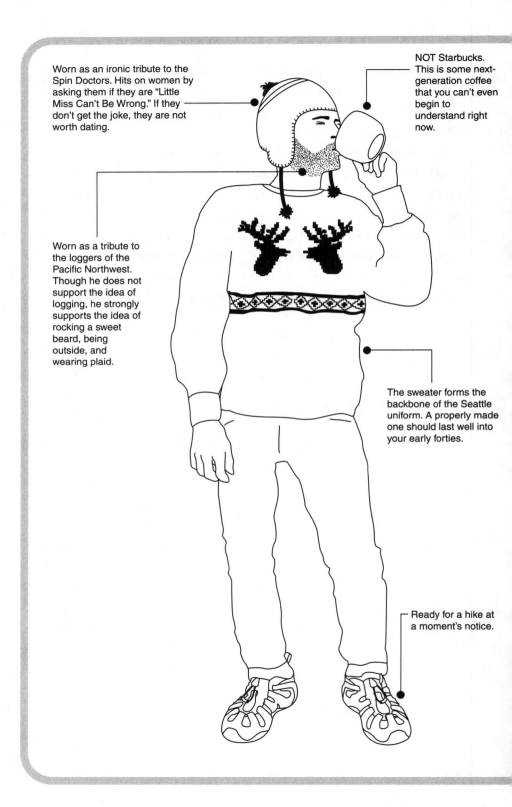

Worn as an ironic tribute to the Spin Doctors. Hits on women by asking them if they are "Little Miss Can't Be Wrong." If they don't get the joke, they are not worth dating.

NOT Starbucks. This is some next-generation coffee that you can't even begin to understand right now.

Worn as a tribute to the loggers of the Pacific Northwest. Though he does not support the idea of logging, he strongly supports the idea of rocking a sweet beard, being outside, and wearing plaid.

The sweater forms the backbone of the Seattle uniform. A properly made one should last well into your early forties.

Ready for a hike at a moment's notice.

Seattle, Washington

- **Overview** The Seattle white person has long been one of the most visible types of white person. They are generally very friendly, with a passion for all manner of outdoor activities, including kayaking, hiking, and skiing. One of their great faults, however, is the inability to let go of the fact that Nirvana may not have been as important as they like to believe. When talking to a Seattle white person about music, it's best to let them believe that their city's relevance extended well beyond a brief period from 1991 to 1994.

- **Strengths** Access to coffee; cardiovascular strength from outdoor activities; sweater thickness.

- **Weaknesses** The sun; mercury poisoning.

- **Secret Shame** The Spin Doctors.

49 | Sweaters

The sweater is an essential part of the white person wardrobe, so it is a very good idea to familiarize yourself with the different types of sweaters that are the most popular with white people.

When you approach the subject from the perspective of age, it's essential that you combine very young and very old white people in the same group. This is because young white people think it is very cool to wear clothes that are popular with senior citizens. The most popular example of this is the cardigan sweater, which is essentially a wool jacket with fewer buttons. An old white person might combine this sweater with a button-down shirt to provide himself or herself with valuable warmth in the winter months, but a young white person will combine it with a T-shirt to create a "layered look." This not only allows them to show others that their personality features as many layers as their clothes, it is also a chance to show people that they own not one but two cool items of clothing.

White women will also purchase many small, thin sweaters that they can wear in combination with or on top of other clothes. Though you may think it would make more sense to just purchase a thicker sweater, these layers are considered to be stylish and they allow their wearers to achieve maximum temperature control.

Moving up in thickness and age, there is also the "ultrathick" sweater. Though you will find these at farmer's markets and community gardens throughout the country, they are most popular in the Pacific Northwest. These are often light brown or almost beige and weigh upwards of ten pounds. When you a see a white person walk into a bar or coffeeshop wearing one of these sweaters, you can tell how heavy it is by how much they are sweating when they take it off.

White people also appreciate the irony of ugly sweaters that usually feature things like reindeer and snowmen. (See page 77 for details on Ugly Sweater Parties.)

But regardless of the type of sweater, it is also good to be aware of the fact that finding a nice sweater at a thrift shop or Goodwill is considered a major event in the life of a white person. Scoring a quality garment that makes it into the regular rotation for under $10 is a story that white people will tell for up to five years after it happens. Therefore, if you are seeking white friendship it is a good idea to do one of two things: go to dozens of thrift shops in hopes of finding a dream sweater, or buy a new one, remove the label, and make up a story about how you found it at a Goodwill in a bad neighborhood that "hadn't been picked clean by hipsters."

50 | Christopher Guest Movies

Christopher Guest is a famous director who has made such movies as *Waiting for Guffman*, *A Mighty Wind*, and *Best in Show*. He also co-wrote and acted in a movie called *This Is Spinal Tap*, which is generally regarded as one of the most popular movies in all of white history.

His film style is often described as "mockumentary." Basically it's just like a documentary except that it is perfectly acceptable—and in fact encouraged—to laugh at the pretentious protagonists. The same actions that would get you kicked out of a home screening of *Food, Inc.* will get you invited back for a screening of *A Mighty Wind*.

Waiting for Guffman is about a small-town production of a play, *Best in*

Show is about people who compete in dog shows, and *A Mighty Wind* looks at folk musicians.

These movies are so beloved by white people because they make fun of people who take things too far. However, determining where exactly that line is can be fraught with danger and consequences. So while it's okay to laugh at a white person who enters their dog in a dog show, it is *not* okay to laugh at a white person who refers to their dog as a child and treats it as such. It is acceptable to laugh at a white person who is taking their small-town theater production very seriously, but it is *not* acceptable to laugh at someone's child who is taking their first off-Broadway production seriously.

When it comes to folk music, it's okay to laugh at everyone. Even the most serious of white people recognize what a mistake that was.

Rather than try to add to the comedy of these movies, your best bet around white people is to simply profess your love for all that Christopher Guest has done. If you want to take it to the next level, you should casually say, "I heard Christopher Guest is going to be directing an indie version of *Spinal Tap;* it's set in Portland."

You might want to keep a brown paper bag nearby for the inevitable hyperventilation that will follow this announcement.

51 | Offices with Open Floor Plans

At around fifteen years old, white people begin to develop a crushing fear of the work cubicle. Their first viewing of the film

Office Space (and all white people like this movie) only reinforces this crippling fear. Eventually they promise that they will never end up trapped inside its partition walls. Instead they will be an artist, musician, comedian, or some combination of the three.

But as they get a little older and realize that they will need money for the things that they like, they begin to take jobs in fields like advertising, media, technology, and law. Though all these jobs feature tasks that used to be easily accomplished in a cubicle environment, white people feel much better about doing the work if they can do it in an office with an open floor plan.

To a white person, spending time filing expense reports, writing emails, and working on spreadsheets within a cubicle is considered "mind-numbing drudgery." But performing the exact same tasks in an open office with exposed beams and a concrete floor is considered "creative."

Yet when white people begin working for a company with one of these floor plans, they spend their time fantasizing about moving to one of the offices that ring the main workspace. If only they had that office, then they would have some privacy, they could make phone calls, and people couldn't look at their screen. In other words, all of the benefits of working in a cubicle.

If you plan to start a business where you will likely have to employ white people, an open floor plan will give your employees a feeling of creativity in the office. But more important, they will take a pay cut for the privilege.

52 | Small-Batch Soda

You have probably noticed that white people have had a long love affair with diet soda. It has been said that no white person has ordered a full-calorie soda (outside of kosher and Mexican versions) in more than twenty years. For some reason white people are petrified of the processed sweeteners in these sodas, but have no objections to the myriad of chemicals that go into making a Diet Coke a calorie-free beverage.

If you don't believe this fact, put a Big Mac and a plate full of cocaine in front of a white person and observe which one disappears first.

This is because when it comes down to it, white people are more afraid of weight gain than they are of chemicals.

However, recently white people have been willing to make the shift back to full-calorie soda, provided that it meets certain requirements. It must come in a bottle, not a can; it must use real sugar; it must come from a city where white people want to live; it must be produced by an independent company; and it must be considerably more expensive than regular soda. If a soda can meet all of these requirements, it is deemed acceptable and will be stocked as a cold option at locally owned coffeeshops throughout the country.

Note: These white people win everything.

Portland, Oregon

- **Overview** White people in Portland are predominantly made up of creative young professionals who mostly work freelance. While this is generally referred to as having a "career" in Portland, the rest of the country generally refers to it as "unemployment." Portland also has an exceptionally large amount of white people who timed the real estate market in California well enough that they don't really have to work. Their exceptional amount of free time allows Portlanders to devote more time to repairing old record players, converting old bicycles into fixed-gear bikes, and not vaccinating their children.

- **Strengths** Strong legs from bicycling; well read thanks to Powell's; good taste in music.

- **Weaknesses** Polio, measles, rubella, and mumps.

- **Secret Shame** Once bought a book from a shop other than Powell's.

WARNING: Do not tell any Portland white person that you are from California. They will hate you.

53 | Black Music That Black People Don't Listen to Anymore

All musical genres go through a very similar life cycle: birth, growth, mainstream acceptance, decline, and finally obscurity. With black music, however, the final stage is never reached because white people work tirelessly to keep it alive. Once a musical style has lost its relevance with its intended nonwhite audience, it becomes *more* relevant to white people.

Historically speaking, the music white people have kept on life support for the longest period of time is jazz. Thanks largely to public radio, bookstores, and coffeeshops, jazz has carved out a niche in white culture that is not yet ready to be replaced by indie rock. The biggest role that jazz plays in white culture is in the white fantasy of the preferred way to spend leisure time. Or, to be more specific: all white people believe that they prefer listening to jazz over watching television. This is not true.

Every few months, a white person will test this preferred relaxation technique by putting on some jazz and pouring a glass of wine or scotch and telling themselves how nice it is. Then they will get bored and watch television or write emails to other white people about how nice it was to listen to jazz at home. "Last night, I poured myself a glass of Shiraz and put Charlie Parker on the Bose. It was so relaxing, I wish I had a fireplace." Listing this activity as one of your favorites is a surefire way to make progress toward a romantic relationship with a white person.

Along with jazz, white people have also taken quite a shine to the blues, an art form that captured the pain of the black experience in America. In the 1960s, a bunch of British bands started to play their own version of the music and white people have been loving it ever since. (It makes sense. After all, the British were the ones responsible for the creation of the blues in the seventeenth century, or more accurately, they were responsible for the conditions that created said blues.)

Today, white people keep the blues going strong by taking vacations to Memphis, forming awkward bands, making documentaries, and organizing folk festivals. Blues and jazz appeal mostly to older white people and a select few young ones who probably wear fedoras. But that doesn't mean that young white people aren't working hard to preserve music that has lost its cultural relevance. No, there are literally thousands of white people who are giving their all to keep old-school hip-hop alive. Even as you read this, white people are telling other white people about the golden age of hip-hop that they experienced at their suburban high school or when they watched *The Wackness*.

If you are good at concealing laughter and contempt, you should ask a white person about "real hip-hop." They will quickly tell you about how they don't listen to "commercial hip-hop" (music that black people actually enjoy) and how they much prefer "classic hip-hop."

"I don't listen to that commercial stuff. I'm more into the real hip-hop, you know? KRS-One, Del Tha Funkee Homosapien, De La Soul, Wu Tang. You know, the old school."

Calling this style of music "old school" is especially apt since the majority of people who listen to it did so while attending old schools such as Dartmouth, Bard, and Williams.

What it all comes down to is that white people are convinced that if they had been alive when this music was relevant they would have been into it. They would have been Alan Lomax or Rick Rubin. Now the best they can hope for is to impress an older black person who liked this music when it was actually popular with black people.

54 Bob Marley

During the course of a white person's education they will go through many phases, including but not limited to "awkward," "classic rock," and "being really into a foreign country." Of these phases, there is only one that all white people are required to go through before they can obtain their bachelor's degree. It is known as "Bob Marley."

Depending on the coolness of the white person, they can experience this stage anywhere between the sixth grade and their last year of college. Regardless of when they went through this phase, every white person can tell you about the time when they had *Legend* on repeat. If you wish to test this theory, go to any floor in a college dorm and there is a 100 percent chance you will find at least one Bob Marley poster.

It is also worth noting that white people tend to get into smoking marijuana during this phase. This is why all white people view the combination of Marley and marijuana as one of the most pleasurable experiences on earth. But when white people really want to take it to the next level, they will combine Bob Marley, marijuana, a long weekend, and some sort of notable outdoor location (beach, cottage, or patio). There are few activities on earth that are more appealing to white people.

The only acceptable reasons for declining participation are a prior engagement at a music festival and a commitment to go camping.

It's also worth noting that when talking to white people about Bob

Marley there is no need to use his surname. This is because all white people refer to him simply as "Bob."

Since so many people are into Bob Marley, it is only natural for advanced white people to profess to only marginally liking Bob Marley (note: it is impossible for a white person to outright dislike him). Instead these white people will claim to prefer more obscure artists like Burning Spear or Peter Tosh.

But be warned that when a white person says they like "reggae" what they really mean is "reggae from 1965 to 1983." Under no circumstances should you ever bring a white person to a dance hall reggae concert. It will frighten them.

Note: If you are talking to a white person who is really into Bob Marley, has dreadlocks, and professes to be a Rastafarian, you should end the conversation immediately. These people are of no value unless you need directions to a WTO protest or have questions about how bad a human can smell.

55 Road Trips

White people love all activities that might enable them to "find themselves." Trips to India or wine country, going back to school, doing or not doing something for a year, eating ethnic food, cooking, and so forth are just some of the many examples of white people finding themselves in hopes that the discovery will one day lead to a book deal or screenplay.

But among young white people, no method of finding themselves is more popular than the road trip. In fact, road trips provide white people with the only known practical application of an iPod loaded with two weeks' worth of music.

Some of the more common destinations or reasons for a road trip include skiing, visiting a friend, music festivals, re-creation of Jack Kerouac's *On the Road*, spring break, or driving a friend to college or graduate school.

Regardless of the destination, there are some rules about road trips that must be followed. Chain hotels and restaurants are to be avoided at all costs, the only places to meet crazy characters are in local bars or truck stop diners, an ironic trinket of some sort must be purchased as a memento of the trip, and, finally, moments of silence on the trip are to be used to look out the window and think about important things. These important things include the future, "what it all means," exes, and high school. As a rule, they cannot be thinking about other people unless it relates directly back to the thinker.

After all, what's the point of going on a trip of self-discovery if you spend all your time thinking about how to help other people?

These road trips become important in the development of white people and are often remembered fondly for generations. However, the ultimate road trip is completed by white males between the ages of eighteen and thirty. This trip involves visiting every major-league baseball park in one summer. It is rumored that one in every fifteen white males has accomplished this feat.

56 Not Vaccinating Children

From your observations, you might assume that by nature of their birthright white children are automatically vaccinated against many things: poverty, public schools, sweatpants, and high-fructose corn syrup. Because of this, it's easy to think that they would all be given some sort of superdrug that would prevent them from getting diseases like polio, measles, mumps, or rubella. You know, the type of thing that millions of poor children around the world are literally dying to get in their home country.

But you would be wrong.

For a few years now, white people have been resisting the idea of getting their children vaccinated against the diseases that brought suffering to millions and were wiped out by modern medicine. Their logic follows a number of paths. The first is a need to get back to our natural state, specifically the one that is vulnerable to the diseases that killed off many of our ancestors. Though their life expectancy might have only been twenty-six, it was a wonderful twenty-six years, filled with organic, whole-grain misery.

The other bit of white logic involves a single now-discredited doctor writing a paper that claimed vaccinations lead to autism. Couple this with

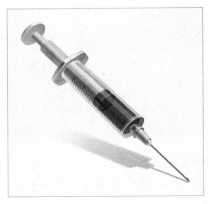

a few equally misinformed celebrity endorsements and that's all white people needed to freak out.

They will feel no discomfort or guilt about sending their little host to school with children who are vaccinated. On the surface, their reasoning will be that since all the other kids are vaccinated, then all the children are safe. But deep down they are secretly hoping that all the vaccinated children have "caught" autism, and that their child will be virtually guaranteed that top-of-the-class ranking.

It goes without saying that befriending a white parent with nonvaccinated children has few perks. The only benefit is that you can openly plan and discuss multifamily vacations to pretty much anywhere on earth and not invite the nonvaccinated family. If they ask why they weren't invited you simply need to say, "I heard Vegas just had an outbreak of rubella, sorry. Maybe you could get one of those bubbles for Oliver. Oh yeah, I forgot they have BPH in them."

Expensive vintage glasses purchased with money from a three-month freelance gig at Google.

Store-bought, but she has plans to take up knitting "as soon as life calms down."

Actually Asian, because you don't have to be white, you just have to be rich.

Friends requested that she cook them an "authentic" Asian meal, but the list of dietary requirements forced her to simply grab something from the Whole Foods salad bar.

WHOLE FOODS

San Francisco, California

- **Overview** White people from San Francisco will be the first to tell you that they are unique. But what makes them unique is that they aren't all technically white in the racial sense of the word. No, San Francisco has the amazing ability to bring in people of all backgrounds and quickly turn them into white people. No wonder it's so popular.

- **Strengths** Wealthy; knowledgeable about art and architecture; strong legs due to hills.

- **Weaknesses** Perpetual white guilt.

- **Secret Shame** Scared of Oakland.

WARNING: Never remind white people from San Francisco that the most culturally relevant part of their city is the suburbs.

57 | Girls with Bangs

If you see a white woman and you are trying to figure out whether she is liked or just merely tolerated by white people, the best thing you can do is get a quick look at her haircut. It is a known fact that white people love women who wear their hair with bangs that hang straight down.

A number of very popular white women have worn this hairstyle, including Joni Mitchell, Jane Birkin, Zooey Deschanel, Jenny Lewis, and every girl ever photographed by *Vice* magazine or the Cobrasnake. (Note: It is a good idea to familiarize yourself with both of the latter, as they are beloved by cool white people. Follow-up note: These same things are despised by cooler white people.)

Many people associate this type of haircut with children and people looking for the most efficient way to get their hair out of their eyes. But for white people, this simple haircut is a bold declaration: the wearer is artistic, deep,

and has probably dated a guy in a band you like. Of course, as with many things loved by white people, simple often means expensive; these haircuts almost always cost upwards of $100.

It is essential for you to understand that this haircut is more than a mere fashion statement—it is an important cultural marker. Throughout the world, many cultures feature ceremonies to announce that a girl has become a woman. For white people, the haircut with bangs symbolizes that a female has completed her transformation from a nerdy girl to a cool woman. In fact, if you went to high school with a nerdy white girl who moved to a big city, there is a good chance she will show up at your high school reunion with bangs.

When you are introduced to a group of white people, it's a good idea to befriend the girl with the bangs. She's probably the most popular.

58 Hating People Who Wear Ed Hardy

Often it can be easier to find common ground with a white person by talking to them about something you both hate. Discussing things you both like might lead to an argument over who likes it more or who liked it first. Clearly the safest route is mutual hatred. When choosing to talk about something that white people hate, it's best to choose something that will allow white people to make clever comments

or at the very least feel better about themselves. Currently the easiest way to do that is to ask a white person for their thoughts on people who wear Ed Hardy.

Ed Hardy is a clothing company that makes a wide range of expensive T-shirts, hoodies, and jeans. These clothes are notable for their use of elements from classic tattoo design such as

skulls, hearts, and dragons. On the surface, the use of the words *classic*, *tattoo*, and *T-shirt* would suggest a logical fit for white people, but that's not the case. The right kind of white people hate these clothes unilaterally, and it is advised that you merely accept that at face value. If you were to ask a white person to explain why a regular-size dragon logo is okay but one that goes around the neck is not, you would be trapped in a long and fruitless conversation.

To put this in proper perspective, Ed Hardy is so hated by white people that it cannot be worn ironically. This is no small feat. As it stands, the only other entries in this category are Nazi uniforms, Ku Klux Klan robes, and self-tanner.

Since you cannot in good conscience have an Ed Hardy–themed party, the best way to make use of this white hatred is to give your stories a little more appeal to white people.

For example, if you take the reasonable but not compelling story "I got cut off in traffic this morning and when I honked the guy gave me the finger" and replace it with "I got cut off in traffic this morning by this guy in an Ed Hardy shirt; I honked and then he gave me the finger!" the story will become 60 percent more interesting to white people because it allows them to make a witty response like "I guess that douche bag had to get to a UFC party or a nightclub event he was promoting."

Follow this up with a laugh, a high-five, and a compliment about the acceptable shirt the white person is wearing, and you will find yourself with a new friend.

59 | Swimming

Among the physical activities most enjoyed by white people, swimming remains right near the top. In fact swimming is the one activity that remains constant throughout the life of a white person. They begin with swim lessons as a child, join a swim team in high school, train for a triathlon after college, and then swim as a way to stay in shape after fifty. If you ask any white person over sixty how they stay in shape, the answer will inevitably be "swimming laps." Or perhaps more accurately, "swimming laps in a Speedo."

It is hard to say exactly why white people love swimming so much, but there are a number of theories. First, all of the great tragedies to befall white people in the water were brought about by white people, shark attacks, getting lost at sea, and the *Titanic*. (Though the latter was technically a tragedy brought about by an iceberg, it was still a white iceberg that did it.) Aside from these minor hiccups, swimming has been a pleasurable activity for white people for generations.

Another theory of why white people enjoy swimming so much is their ability to completely dominate the sport. Of course, this domination doesn't come from years of training and crushing competition; it owes mostly to the fact that white people only have to compete against other white people. This is in turn because even at the highest levels, nonwhite competitors are mostly limited to a few overeager Chinese Olympians or

some adorable underdog from a third-world country who just learned to swim.

Swimming at the Olympics is actually another example of how good white people are at figuring out how to maximize the few ways in which they can eke out athletic dominance. White people have helped to ensure that you can win medals in swimming for different distances, relays, and, most important, different strokes. So white athletes can win upwards of five medals for doing the butterfly and the backstroke, but in track, a sport long abandoned by white people, they could not obtain additional medals for running backward or doing a crab walk.

Sadly there seems to be no end in sight for white people's dominance of competitive swimming. For further proof, go to the nearest computer and type in "swim team" on Google. Then click on the "Images" tab. You will see more white flesh than in a Mormon orgy.

Competition and pleasure are logical reasons why white people would enjoy swimming, but these are not the only factors that will put people in the water. Many white people will engage in something called "polar bear" events, where they gather on a beach in the middle of winter, quickly jump into a partially frozen lake or ocean, and then run back to waiting blankets and warm beverages. This is often done to remind white people they are alive. For white people, nothing makes them appreciate the gift of life more than voluntarily trying to end it.

60 | Google

Thanks to a middle school reading of the book *1984*, virtually all white people have an intense fear of a "big brother" type of organization that monitors all your actions and compiles terabytes of data on you, your family, and all your actions. A white person can think of nothing more frightening than some strange company holding all of their information and using it for their own benefit. That is, unless that company happens to be Google—then everything is fine.

White people have spent the past decade happily handing over as much of their life as possible to Google: email, work documents, video chat, payment systems, news sources, and all of their Internet searches. If Google offered to digitize and store all financial and medical records, white people would be among the first to jump aboard, partly because this would

make dating much easier for white people, because the ability to use your phone to view a sexual history report and a 401(k) statement could save you hours of indirect, veiled questions.

There are a number of reasons white people have been so eager to hand over their lives to Google. The first and most obvious reason is simple peer pressure. If you've ever exchanged email with a white person there is a 100 percent chance their email address ended in @gmail.com. Of course, some white people have an @mac.com address, but even those people know that they'll need an @gmail.com address if they want anyone to take them seriously. (See pages 71–72 for examples of what can happen when you don't have the right email address.)

But one of the biggest reasons why white people love Google is simply the company itself. It is famous for providing its employees with all sorts of perks like free food, ball pits, arcade machines, and pretty much anything else that will take the misery out of coding for eighteen hours a day.

Finally, Google is renowned for having a very selective hiring process that enables them to bring on only the best and brightest people on earth. So naturally, every white person believes that they should be working there. When a white person with a job that you covet begins complaining, simply tell them that they should be working at Google. The pull of dot-com money, endless perks, and working in a selective environment will be too strong and they will immediately begin searching for a job. While they are filling out Google's strange questionnaire, inform your superior that the white person is looking for a new job, and enjoy your new promotion!

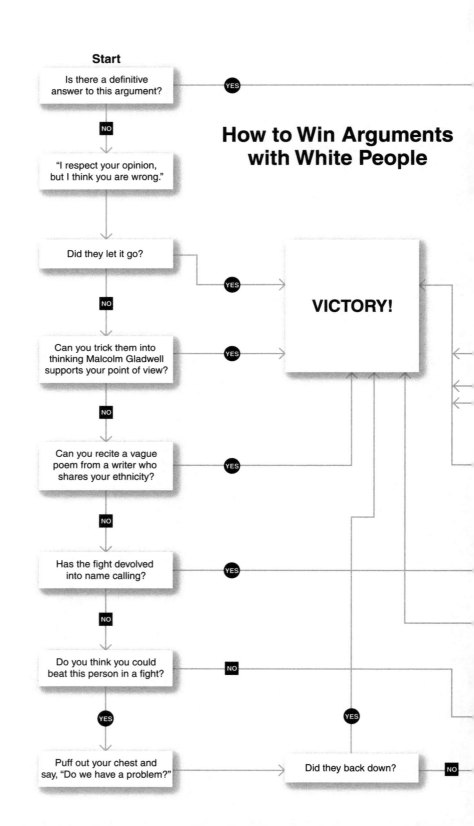

How to Win Arguments with White People

Start

Is there a definitive answer to this argument? — **YES**

NO

"I respect your opinion, but I think you are wrong."

Did they let it go? — **YES** → **VICTORY!**

NO

Can you trick them into thinking Malcolm Gladwell supports your point of view? — **YES** →

NO

Can you recite a vague poem from a writer who shares your ethnicity? — **YES**

NO

Has the fight devolved into name calling? — **YES**

NO

Do you think you could beat this person in a fight? — **NO**

YES

Puff out your chest and say, "Do we have a problem?" → Did they back down? — **NO**

YES

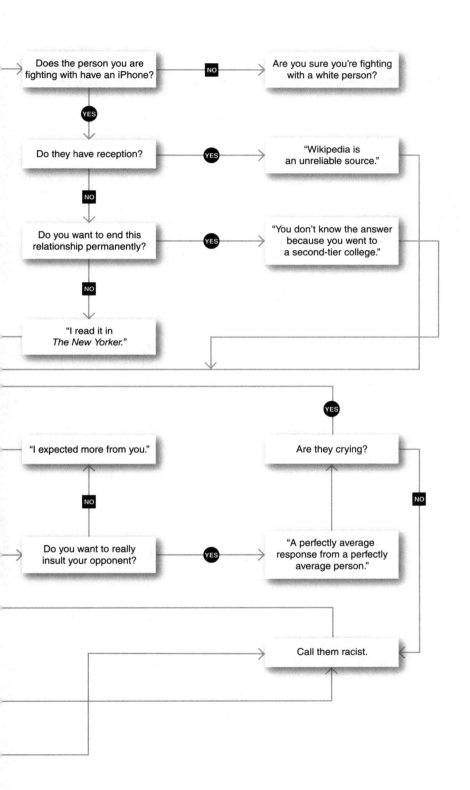

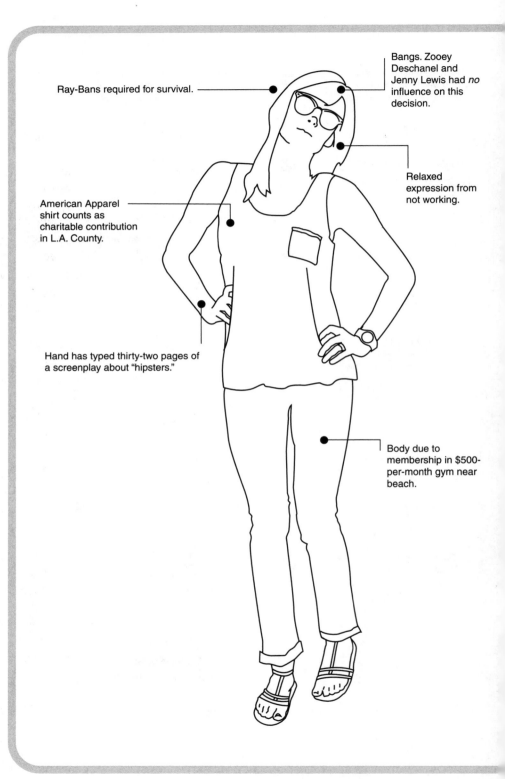

Ray-Bans required for survival.

Bangs. Zooey Deschanel and Jenny Lewis had *no* influence on this decision.

Relaxed expression from not working.

American Apparel shirt counts as charitable contribution in L.A. County.

Hand has typed thirty-two pages of a screenplay about "hipsters."

Body due to membership in $500-per-month gym near beach.

Los Angeles, California

- **Overview** The Los Angeles white person spends most of their time focused on interior design, yoga, and pretending to be a part of the entertainment industry. They are easily identified by their brightly colored Ray-Ban Wayfarers and their worship of cultish chefs.

- **Strengths** Can probably get you tickets to Coachella; knows how to drive.

- **Weaknesses** Crippling debt; insecurity; might ask you to read screenplay.

- **Secret Shame** Reality television legally eliminated the concept of shame from Los Angeles County in 2004.

WARNING: Never tell a Los Angeles white person that quality Mexican food can exist outside the city of Los Angeles. This could end your friendship permanently.

61 | *Mad Men*

Television is one of the keys to a white person's heart. A proper reference to *Arrested Development* and the lending of a *Wire* season on DVD are considered two of the easiest and most cost-effective ways of getting a white person to like you. But with both of those shows off the air, their utility is being quickly depleted. Thankfully, there is *Mad Men*.

Mad Men is a TV show on cable with low ratings, multiple awards, critical praise, and full seasons available on DVD. It's no surprise white people love it. And while you could apply the previously mentioned techniques to gain white friendship, *Mad Men* offers an entirely new world of possibilities.

The show is set in the early 1960s and features meticulous art direction that strives to make the show as historically accurate as possible. This veracity makes the show especially vulnerable to one of white people's favorite activities on earth: finding mistakes. And as is always the case with white people, the harder someone strives for accuracy, the happier a white person is to prove them wrong.

"Oh yeah, it's a great show, don't get me wrong. But you'd think at least one person would have known that those IBM Selectric typewriters didn't come out until 1961. I mean, it's so obvious."

But it is not recommended that you start searching for mistakes on the show. Doing so would require spending a massive amount of time on the Internet. Also, if you point out errors that other white people missed, they might be intimidated by you.

Instead, the best way to use *Mad Men* is to suggest or host a themed party.

When you say the words "We should have a *Mad Men* party," white people will immediately latch on to the idea and begin planning. By the end of the day, they will have picked proper attire and emailed you a drink and hors d'oeuvre menu. In the days and weeks leading up to the party, white people will be thinking of clever ways to make the party as authentic as possible.

Remember, parties are fun, but historically accurate themed parties are legendary.

During the actual event you should constantly mention how much people used to smoke and drink back then. A few white people will lament the days when they could smoke anywhere, then another white person will say something about cancer and it will get awkward. At this point you should try to steer the conversation back to cocktails and how good everyone looks in their vintage clothes.

The party should essentially run itself. However, you can severely curtail the amount of fun by saying, "I'm glad this isn't really 1960 or else I'd be serving all of you."

White people often find truth to be very depressing at themed parties.

62 Ray-Ban Wayfarers

White people can do powerful things with their eyes: cast judgment, indicate scorn, and obnoxiously roll them when someone says something they don't agree with. Yet in spite of these powers, they are not immune to the dangers of the sun. White people must wear sunglasses. But what may surprise you is that while white people will spend upwards of three months finding a perfect pair of unique prescription frames, they have no such requirement for sunglasses.

Right now, all white people are either wearing or coveting a pair of Ray-Ban Wayfarer sunglasses.

These sunglasses are so popular now that you cannot swing a canvas bag at a farmer's market without hitting a pair. In fact, at outdoor gatherings you should count the number of Wayfarers so you can determine exactly how white the event is. If you see no Wayfarers you are either at a country music concert or you are indoors.

White people love these Ray-Bans because they were very popular in the 1960s and the 1980s. This gives them a historical relevance and allows white people to classify them as "timeless." That way when they purchase these sunglasses they can talk about how they were inspired by the fashion and music of these bygone eras. When a white person says this, you should just nod and mention how they look like a young Johnny Cash, a dead Beach Boy, Audrey Hepburn, or an extra from a John Hughes movie. This will make them happy and likely to give you their old expensive sunglasses, which you can sell for profit.

Under no circumstances should you imply that white people purchased their sunglasses because of celebrities who are not dead or because they saw them on other white people they think are cool. This will make them very upset. White people need to believe that they cannot be persuaded to do anything.

A statement like "Man, it's pretty amazing how sixty-five people at this outdoor concert all decided to get their sunglasses at exactly the same time" should only be directed at a white person who is not wearing Wayfarers. This will make them feel better about not fitting in, but it will also make them self-conscious about their plan to buy a pair.

Note: A significant number of white women are still wearing oversize sunglasses, but they are a dying breed.

63 *My So-Called Life*

Though very specific to white people who were going through an awkward phase in 1995 (basically anyone between eleven and forty), *My So-Called Life*'s resonance cannot be overstated. Simply say the words *Jordan Catalano*. Say them to any white woman, gay white male, or superconfident-in-his-sexuality, irony-loving straight white male, and watch them swoon.

You seriously do not even need an explanation about the show. Actually, if someone asks your name, you should say it's Jordan Catalano and that you've never heard of the show. You

will be the hit of the party, provided you let everyone in on the joke by the middle of the evening. Otherwise you will probably be known as a self-centered, dyslexic jerk.

The show itself was seen as revolutionary for its frank and honest dealings with same-sex relationships, drug and alcohol use among teenagers, and domestic abuse. However, the part of the show that truly bonds white people together is not their common experience of exploring these issues. No, it's the collective sense of regret for mid-nineties fashion.

"Do you remember the episode where Rayanne had the drug overdose?"

"Sort of. Do you remember that choker necklace she wore? What were we thinking?"

"I've actually had a drug prob—"

"And the scrunchies? Are you kidding me?"

So rather than attempting to use the social aspect of the show to forge a deep connection with white people, you should simply revert to the number-one rule when dealing with white people: throw a themed party.

As a male, if you arrive with a white T-shirt, ripped jeans, and a plaid shirt tied around your waist you should be guaranteed, at the very least, a make-out session. As a female, show up with a plaid skirt, combat boots, and your hair parted down the middle. Though this outfit would normally get you branded as a lesbian, tonight it will have quite the opposite effect.

Note: You may notice that all the music from this era is very depressing. Do not worry about it having a negative effect on your party. White people have an amazing ability to get drunk and then all happily sing, in unison, a song about suicide.

64 The Huffington Post

There are few things white people like more than being told that they were right. In fact for most white people this is the sole reason they are so excited to attend high school reunions. Unfortunately, the opportunity to show that you made the right choice in eating habits, proper age to have children, college degree, and clothing comes along but once every ten years.

So white people are instead forced to look for simple, more replicable ways to be reminded of their correctness. For many of them, simply moving to Northern California; Boulder, Colorado; Madison, Wisconsin; or Portland, Oregon, will accomplish this task permanently, since literally everything accomplished in those places is a constant reminder that white people are right.

But in the wide-open world of the Internet, there are so many dissenting points of view that it can be hard to find one single place where white people can be reassured that their view is the best one. Sure, they could try *The New York Times*, NPR, or even Rachel Maddow, but all of those sources are required to show at least some level of journalistic integrity, which is defined by white people as "allowing conservatives to speak."

Since its inception, the best place for white people to find political and cultural affirmation is The Huffington Post. This website features

everything white people are looking for in one easy location: editorials, clips from *The Daily Show*, and slide shows that will provide white people with tens of minutes of dinner party conversation about the ten best cities for creative people.

But the best thing about The Huffington Post is that it covers politics and celebrities with just about equal zeal. This means white people can pretend to be reading about a regime change in Afghanistan when a co-worker walks by, and then quickly scroll down to a story about a celebrity DUI. This enables you to appear smart while engaging in something that is probably making you dumber, sort of like the old trick of putting a magazine inside a textbook to trick teachers.

If you plan on using The Huffington Post as a conversation starter, do not go straight into celebrity news. White people know this is a trick. Instead you should reference one of the editorials featured on the site. But don't go too highbrow and reference an editorial by a writer or a former politician. Go for something safer, something the white person has read.

"Did you read the editorial in the HuffPo about the immigration law in Arizona?"

[Awkward pause.]

"The one by Alec Baldwin?"

"Oh yes! It was fantastic!"

Now, rather than trying to move the conversation to the issue, which would require context and some level of reading, simply shift the conversation over to the celebrity and voilà! You have a new best friend who thinks this is a conversation about politics.

> "Do you remember when Alec Baldwin yelled at his kid and everyone heard it?"
> "That was insane. He's so good on *30 Rock*."
> "Yeah."
> "I'm glad we had this talk. I feel like I was on *Charlie Rose* or something."

Not only have you raised the self-esteem of a white person, but you can confirm your suspicions about the intellectual hierarchy of your office. Of course, if a white person rebuffs this conversation and mentions something from a printed magazine, be careful. They are your competition.

65 | American Apparel

From a strictly economic viewpoint, the idea of American Apparel seems like it would be a failure: paying above market rate for labor, charging well above your competitors' prices for the same product, and offering no distinguishing features from the competition. But they made one important decision that virtually guaranteed success: they sold self-satisfaction to white people.

On the white people commodities market, only organic produce sells at a higher volume than self-satisfaction. If you look into the footnotes of the business model for Apple Computer you'll see that they actually give the computers away for free; they just charge for the inflated sense of self-worth.

But more important, American Apparel allows white people to wear a

T-shirt without guilt. Yes, that's correct, white people are so filled with guilt about everything that even the act of wearing a T-shirt is enough to generate shame about the conditions of garment workers in third-world countries. Of course, it doesn't fill them with enough guilt to actually do something about it, just enough guilt to ruin their afternoon. So by wearing an American Apparel shirt, they can not only strut around feeling great, but they are given a secret weapon if they ever find themselves needing to ruin the afternoon of another white person.

"Nice shirt, who makes it?"

"Uh, I think it's Fruit of the Loom."

"Did you read the *Harper's* article about the real cost of a two-dollar T-shirt?"

Note: This is an epic move, because not only does it induce guilt about the shirt, it induces guilt about not reading *Harper's Magazine*.

Some of the possible situations where you might need to ruin another white person's afternoon: trying to get a table at a coffeeshop, attempting to steal a girlfriend or boyfriend, or needing to appear intelligent in front of someone else.

The guilt alleviation/application is but one part of the American Apparel empire. Another reason for their success is that they sell shirts with no logos. Just plain, simple shirts. And if there is one thing we've learned about white people, it's that they will pay a lot of money for simplicity.

But the most important thing that American Apparel has done for white culture is its advertising. The ads themselves are seen by white people as a triumph of style and elegance as well as one of the more acceptable forms of pornography for white people. But more important, you will find their ads on almost every indie music blog on the Internet, which means that their advertising budget is subsidizing almost every important part of the white Internet.

Of course, there have been some downsides to the company. American Apparel has been accused of hiring only attractive people (a claim they deny, sort of) and the CEO of the company has found himself in some hot water over alleged sexual harassment. But most white people can forgive that relatively easily, since the order of people that must be protected goes like this:

1. Third-world people
2. Dogs
3. Poor people in the first world
4. Ugly or fat people
5. Good-looking people

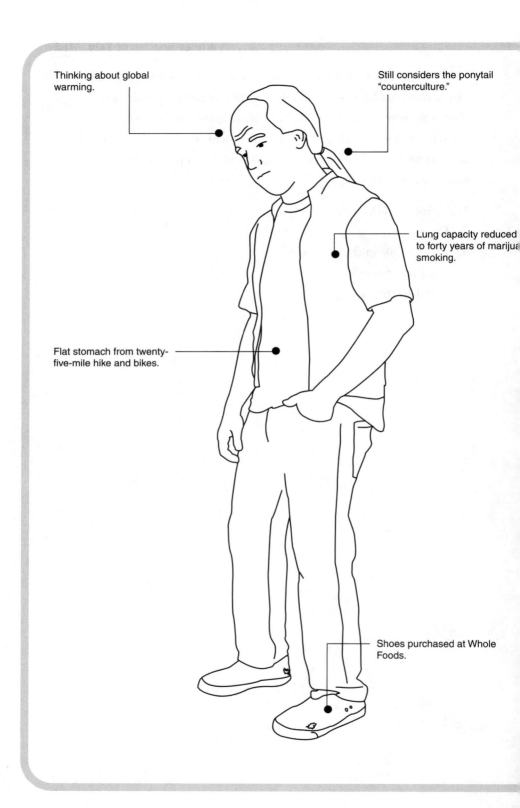

Thinking about global warming.

Still considers the ponytail "counterculture."

Lung capacity reduced to forty years of marijua smoking.

Flat stomach from twenty-five-mile hike and bikes.

Shoes purchased at Whole Foods.

Boulder, Colorado

- **Overview** Nestled in the mountains, Boulder, Colorado, has been singing its siren song to white people for generations. With a college, ample skiing, complete acceptance of hippies, strict development laws, and abundant nature, it's sort of like a halfway house for people who want to move to Canada. The typical Boulder white person is generally older than most, as the only people who can afford to own property in Boulder are those who bought it in the 1970s. They are also in magnificent shape due to Boulder's many bicycle trails and outdoor activities. Additionally, they are very excited about the anticipated arrival of Boulder's first black family, which is currently scheduled for August 2014.

- **Strengths** Wealthy; owns four-wheel-drive automobile.

- **Weaknesses** Frightened when pace of life moves above "casual."

- **Secret Shame** Once heard a Native American tell a story about the creation of earth and thought it was bullshit.

66 Hummus

When it comes to food, all white people are either allergic to or have stopped eating everything you consider delicious. Peanuts, flour, meat, sugar—it's all out. It's a good idea to come to grips with the reality of this now, because it will save you a lot of headaches in the future.

When white people come to your house, you will be forced to deal with the problem in a very real, very immediate sense. You will be limited by their dietary restrictions and they will be limited by the contents of your kitchen. You can mitigate this situation by stocking your pantry with dozens of complicated and expensive snacks. Or you could take the easy way out and just buy a tub of hummus.

All white people like hummus. In fact, if you find a white person who does not like hummus, then they probably just haven't tasted it or they are the wrong kind of white person. In either case they are probably not someone you want to know.

Putting out a plate of hummus and pita makes white people very comfortable. It reminds them of home, since at any given time a white person has hummus in their fridge. Even the most barren white refrigerator will have a package of the stuff next to an empty Brita filter.

White people are also relieved when they see hummus because they instantly know the ingredients and recognize them all as edible. Though you would never be able to guess it by their actions, white people are very concerned with being perceived as "annoying" or "that guy" who has to ask about the ingredients of everything they eat. Yet in spite of this important concern, they are still more afraid of being "that guy" who eats high-fructose corn syrup or pork.

Familiarize yourself with the dietary restrictions of white people, since it will play itself out every time you try to pick a restaurant with a white person.

> **You:** "Let's get Chinese food."
>
> **White Person #1:** "Um, yeah, last time I was there I tried to ask the waitress if they used any pork stock in the preparation of the vegetables and she didn't really give me a response that makes me comfortable eating there again."

By providing your guests with a plate of hummus, you can guarantee that you won't have to have this infuriating conversation in your own home. But that doesn't mean you are safe. To cover all your bases, it is also always a good idea to keep some gluten-free crackers in your pantry. That way if you bring out a plate of hummus and pita and discover that one of the white people cannot eat gluten, you will be ready to pull off a truly incredible move.

First, pretend not to understand why the person cannot eat wheat. Then go back to the kitchen and return with the gluten-free crackers. Everyone will be impressed by your ability to psych out people with food allergies.

Wait one week and relive the story with different white people. It will make them laugh and secretly wish to be invited to your next hummus-eating party.

67 Foreign Military Physical Fitness Regimens

White people believe that everyone else on earth is in better shape than them. Because of this, they are always eager and willing to embrace any exercise fad that comes from a foreign country's military. Though they hate the idea of war and the military-industrial complex, they love the idea of increased lung capacity and solid abs.

In recent years, some popular examples include capoeira (Brazil), Krav Maga (Israel), and kettlebells (Russia). Much in the same way that foreign nations can provide spiritual salvation without a lot of effort (thank you, Buddhism), it is the hope of every white person that they can find a physical fitness equivalent in a foreign military.

Just as white people all hope that becoming a Buddhist involves buying a book and a statue, they hope a new fitness regime will require only a new piece of equipment and maybe a new outfit.

During the first few weeks of this new regimen, white people will not shut up about how great they feel. How they have more energy, feel stronger, and are thinking about moving on to more physically challenging feats such as marathons, hikes, triathlons, or some sort of vacation that involves nothing but exercise.

But don't worry, most white people will just give up after two weeks when they realize that they do not have the chiseled torso of a soldier or the ability to take down a man three times their size. They will have no choice but to quit and wait for the next trend.

If you hope to start one of these trends, it's not very hard. You just have to ask a white person, "Have you ever seen a fat [insert nationality or job]?" And while the reason for the lack of obesity is generally "malnutrition" or "poverty," most white people consider it more logical that the svelte figures are the result of a magic exercise and some sort of tea.

Suggested workout plans: Prison Workout, Day Laborer Fitness Routine, and the Subsistence Farmer Abdominal Shred.

68 Heirloom Tomatoes

The name alone should clue you in to the fact that white people love them. Though it can be very hard to eat "vintage" food due to spoilage, heirloom tomatoes are as close as white people can get.

These tomatoes come from seeds handed down by generations of

farmers and produce tomatoes with no uniformity in color or shape. Essentially each tomato is its own unique and special entity, sort of like a white child—though it should be noted that you should never imply that eating a tomato is in any way similar to eating a white child. The only way to escape from this awkward conversation would be to try to move the conversation to a discussion of

Jonathan Swift, but even that requires the deftest of touches with white people to pull off.

Much in the same way that white people like to be able to trace their pedigree back to the *Mayflower* or (if they are lucky) a Native American, they are very comfortable with the idea that their food can do the same thing. In fact, if you could create a fake document that proved your tomatoes were somehow descended from the farm of George Washington Carver, white people would probably pay $20 per tomato not only for the flavor but for the opportunity to eat progress.

With its advanced pedigree, one-of-a-kind shape and taste, high earning potential, and elevated status at a farmer's market, the heirloom tomato is the food equivalent to everything that white people hope to be. If you present one as a gift to a white person, be sure to mention how much the fruit reminds you of them.

69 | Prescription Drugs

It is a certainty that if you are ever required to go to the hospital for any sort of injury, the first thing that a white person will ask you is which drugs you were given. They won't ask about lingering effects, the quality of care, how it affected your family, your insurance situation—none of that will matter in the face of their curiosity about which drugs you were given.

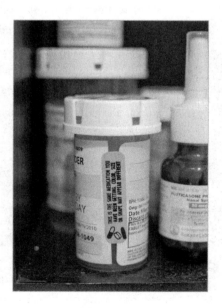

"I hurt my back this weekend. I just got back from the hospit—"

"What drugs did they give you?"

"Vicodi—"

"Oooooooh, do you have any extras? Just kidding, well, not really."

At this point, the white person has essentially asked you to be their drug dealer. If you're not a drug dealer, this is very offensive and it's up to you if you'd like to call this white person racist and enjoy a number of guilt-related gifts and meals. If you *are* a drug dealer, you should not attempt to set up a deal with this person for a larger quantity of pills.

It is the acquisition of the drugs that makes all the difference. White people learned a long time ago that one of the greatest benefits of prescription drugs is that an insurance company will pay for them. So any and all drugs that are paid for by an insurance company are completely acceptable for consumption, including those prescribed to friends and family members.

But if you buy the same drugs on the Internet or from a dealer, then you are most definitely the wrong kind of white person. Unless you were doing it to get on *Intervention* on A&E, and then maybe it's all right, provided you write a memoir, too.

The ability to understand the difference between casual abuse of prescription drugs and problematic abuse of prescription drugs will be of the utmost importance in your friendship with white people. For example, a white person finding an old Vicodin in the medicine cabinet and then washing it down with a glass of vodka and falling asleep listening to an old Pavement CD is considered to be an acceptable activity. A white person buying a Percocet from a drug dealer and then going home, taking it, and falling asleep to a 3 Doors Down album is not acceptable, and an intervention must be performed immediately. This will address the problem of a drug addiction and the far more important problem of appalling taste in music.

70 | Olives

There are few fruits or vegetables that play a more important role in the world of fine dining or dinner party hosting than the olive. Regardless of the size, grade, or pedigree, when white people get together there is an implicit agreement that some form of olive will be made available. This is important should you ever have white guests past 6 P.M.

The exact reason why white people love olives so much has been lost for centuries. There are theories that the popularity is due to the fact that olives require an immense amount of work and energy to create a relatively small result. Much like a nonprofit organization.

But the most important reason you should familiarize yourself with olives is their role as a signifier that your neighborhood is being overrun by white people. No, white people won't start planting olive trees; that would be far too much work. But rather your local supermarket will see the addition of what looks like a pushcart filled with sun-dried tomatoes, cheeses in water, and, of course, olives. This cart arrives because the white people who have moved into this neighborhood have accumulated enough quality furniture (and are confident enough in the crime levels) to host a dinner party. In shopping for that party they realized that the local market didn't carry fresh olives and they quickly escalated this complaint to the manager. And voilà, olives show up in your supermarket.

On the plus side, when you see those olives you should buy as much property in the neighborhood as you possibly can.

Look of confusion comes from constant question about whether or not he should have gone to law school.

Thinking about dropping out and working in publishing.

Trying to look older, though sadly the thrift store jacket is two years older than him.

Political T-shirt in an attempt to inspire students to stop drinking and start reading books.

Heart still broken from when a student called Nabokov a "homo."

Burning through Victorian novels to show up a rival at an upcoming graduate school party.

Contains thirty-three tests, one copy of Foucault's *Discipline and Punish*, one copy of Barthes's *Mythologies, The New Yorker*, and a hidden copy of Harry Potter.

Proven fact that men in graduate school are attracted to sensible shoes.

College Towns Throughout the United States

- **Overview** This type of white person can be found in literally any college town in the United States. They can often blend seamlessly into any university community, and they often have near rabid fanaticism for indie rock, art house cinema, and HBO-produced television series. They can be found at the library or desperately trying to befriend the proprietor of one of the few ethnic restaurants available in their small town.

- **Strengths** Smart (sort of); well read; opinionated.

- **Weaknesses** Self-induced poverty; depression; reliance on free food at university functions for sustenance.

- **Secret Shame** Did not correct fellow grad student for mixing up Marcuse and Lacan.

71 | Facebook

Social networking sites have been embraced by white people since their inception. Because these sites use profile pages, white people can more efficiently judge friends and future friends on their taste in film, books, music, and inspirational quotes. Advanced-level white people, fearful of being judged on their tastes from last week, will often only list one or two ironic things as their favorites. For example, under music they would simply list P.M. Dawn or under films they would choose only *Armageddon*. In both cases these ironic answers serve as protective shields from the harsh gaze of other white people.

However, it is important to remember that the "where" is often as important as the "who" when it comes to social networking. As noted earlier, white people are obsessed with being in the right neighborhood, and the Internet is no exception.

In the early days, white people joined a social networking service called Friendster, where they could connect with old friends and make new ones. Eventually white people started to notice more and more of their friends on MySpace, so they closed their Friendster accounts and migrated to the new service. It was like living in a neighborhood that was pretty good but kind of far away, so you might have to miss out on a few parties. Needless to say, this was unacceptable.

For a brief period of time, MySpace was the site where everyone kept their profiles and managed their friendships. But soon the service began to attract fake profiles, the wrong kind of white people, and struggling musicians. In real-world terms, these three developments would be equivalent to a check-cashing store, a T.G.I. Friday's, and a housing project. All of which strike fear in the hearts of white people.

White people were nervous but had nowhere else to go. Then Facebook came along and offered advanced privacy settings, closed networks, and a clean interface. In respective real-world terms, these features are analogous to a house or apartment with a security system/doorman, an alumni dinner, and a homeowners association that guarantees the protection of the aesthetics of the neighborhood. In spite of these advances, some white people still clung to their old MySpace accounts. That is, until they learned that Facebook was started, like so many things beloved by white people, at Harvard.

Within a matter of months, MySpace had gone from a virtual utopia to digital Detroit, where only minorities and indie bands remain.

As it is with almost everything white people like, the advanced white people will of course talk to you about how they are thinking about deleting their Facebook account because of the issue of privacy and the terms of use of the site. What they are really looking for is someone to tell them to keep their account, how enjoyable their updates, photos, and general presence on the site are. It's like wanting to hear your eulogy before your funeral. So while these white people might talk a big game, they aren't actually going to do anything about it.

If you plan on befriending white people, it is essential that you join them in the digital suburbs and open a Facebook account immediately. It's also a good idea to make up a story about how someone from high school sent you a friend request and that after accepting you discovered that they were fat and unsuccessful. White people love these stories.

72 | *Where the Wild Things Are*

It is a guarantee that whenever it is announced that a popular book is being turned into a movie, white people will get upset. This is partly due to their fear that something they love will be made accessible to more people and thus enjoyed by more people, which immediately decreases the amount of joy a white person can feel toward the original property. Yes, it's complicated.

The other problem is that these announcements create a ticking time bomb whereby a white person must read the book in *advance* of the release of the movie. This is done partly so that they can engage in the popular activity of complaining about how the movie failed to capture the essence of the book. But more important, once a book has been made into a movie, a white person can no longer read that book. To have read the book after the movie's release is one of the great crimes in white culture, and under no circumstance should you ever admit to doing this. Literally dozens of white friendships have imploded when it was revealed that someone read *Fight Club* after 1999.

So when it was announced that *Where the Wild Things Are* was being turned into a feature film, white people didn't immediately get excited at the prospect. In fact, a great number of white people cringed when they first heard it was being turned into a movie. This was merely instinct. But those concerns quickly turned into an opiate-like peace when they found out that the film wass being directed by white person favorite Spike Jonze and adapted for the screen by legendary white writer Dave Eggers.

Though the talent and the material have white people in a tizzy, the real excitement comes from the fact that this film is based on a book that is forty-eight pages long and made up mostly of illustrations. This means that white people do not have to reread the book until the day they head to the movie theater. This frees them up to watch the Director's Series, Vol. 1, *The Work of Spike Jonze* DVD that they bought years ago but only watched once.

Finally and perhaps of most value to you is the fact that the film has generously provided you with an excellent way to test out how many white friends you have. When the trailer was released, you should have been inundated with emails, instant messages, and Facebook wall posts about how you need to see the trailer immediately. If you received no word that the trailer was available, then you currently are in possession of no white friends. If you received multiple notices, you should take note of who sent it to you first. They are your whitest friend.

73 | Cult Movies

Cult movies are one of the hardest things to understand about white people. In straightforward terms, white people like movies that are so bad that somehow they eventually come back around to being good. Sort of like how communism and fascism meet at the ends of the political spectrum. Make sense? No, it doesn't. But that's all right. It's a complicated concept and something that is only really understood by those who have reached expert-level status with white people.

It is impossible for a white person to explain the difference between a bad movie and a bad-good movie. This is because all white people are

born with the ability to detect and appreciate high camp. In much the same way that dogs can hear higher frequencies, white people are born with the ability to fully enjoy the works of John Waters.

But do not think that this means a movie is naturally born as a cult classic. No, it must go through a number of steps. The first is to be declared a cult movie by white people who used to work in video stores but now spend most of their time on message boards and hanging around art house cinemas. The second, and more important, step is that a large group screening must be organized and well attended. Once this has happened, a movie is a cult classic and can be enjoyed with popcorn and a detached sense of irony.

Finally, accepting an invitation to go see one of these movies is less an opportunity for fun and more of a sentence to at least a few hours of prep work. You will be expected to pre-watch the movie so you can yell out your favorite lines, and it's sort of implied that you will dress up as one of the characters. Under no circumstance should you ever accept an invitation to go see *The Rocky Horror Picture Show*. White people spend less time preparing for their SATs than they do for this movie.

74 | Long-Distance Relationships

In their twenties and early thirties, many white people will engage in something called a "long-distance relationship," though for brevity's sake it might be easier to think of it as an "extremely slow breakup."

The long-distance relationship generally begins as a short-distance relationship either in college or during a particularly memorable weekend trip somewhere. No matter how it starts, the long-distance relationship begins when one white person moves away from the other. Normal logic would dictate that if you're living in different cities, living different lives, then there really is no point to a relationship and you should just end it now. But not white people.

Regardless of how many of these relationships have failed (an incredible 100 percent), white person logic dictates that you can keep a long-distance relationship alive and healthy by talking on the phone every day and meeting every few weekends. Eventually some amazing coincidence will bring the two back together and everything will work itself out. It should be noted that the influence of romantic comedies on white people has been a decidedly negative one.

Eventually, after an extended period, the relationship will break down when one white person "cheats" on the other. At this point the phone calls will stop and the white person who has been dumped will return to a life where they spend every day without their significant other. In other words, pretty much the exact same scenario they were in during the relationship.

If you are interested in dating a white person who is in one of these long-distance relationships, you will find yourself at a distinct advantage. While other white people will back off out of respect for the institution of the long-distance relationship, you are bound by no such law. If your early advances are rejected by your target, simply wait. The current record for a long-distance relationship is six months.

75 *The Big Lebowski*

When it comes to the Coen brothers, white people can't get enough. Their films are intelligent, complex, brilliantly done, and funny, sort of. You see, these filmmaking brothers often tackle large issues with dense, layered scripts in movies that most white people think are funny, but they can't be sure until they see someone smarter than them laughing at the screen. Fortunately, the Coen brothers made a movie, *The Big Lebowski*, which is the most straightforward funny movie that they have ever made and therefore is the absolute favorite of white people everywhere.

The movie is a modern update on film noir, something that all white people profess to like but don't actually watch. In fact white people generally consider *The Big Sleep* to be the best film that they've never seen.

Most white people will say that they love *The Big Lebowski* because it has good characters, it's quotable, and it's just fantastic filmmaking. But as we've proven time and again, the film simply provides white people with another excuse for themed drinking, specifically White Russians. If you take nothing away from this film, just remember that it is impossible to order this drink without a white person immediately quoting something from the movie.

This probably explains why every time you've had one of these drinks a white person has started yelling at you about Donnie or telling you that the Dude abides. If you happen to have any Spanish blood in you, then a quick quote from the Jesus character played by John Turturro will almost certainly net you a second free drink courtesy of a delighted white person.

The film is also responsible for a significant spike in white people going bowling. The pastime has always been popular with "retro" white people, specifically the women who wear pointy fifties glasses and men who are into tiki bars and Hawaiian shirts. But the pastime was vaulted into the realm of acceptable for millions of white people after the release of the movie. Suggesting a Lebowski night at a local bowling alley is a surefire hit in increasing your popularity with white people.

When you get to the alley you may notice groups of other white people who are dressed in slightly vintage clothes, look stronger than normal white people, and don't smile very often. They are known as "working-class white people" and will probably not be amused by your white friends' clever name for a bowling team. They will probably be even less amused by your white friend who will inevitably show up wearing a bathrobe, shorts, and sunglasses.

On second thought, it's probably just best to avoid this movie altogether.

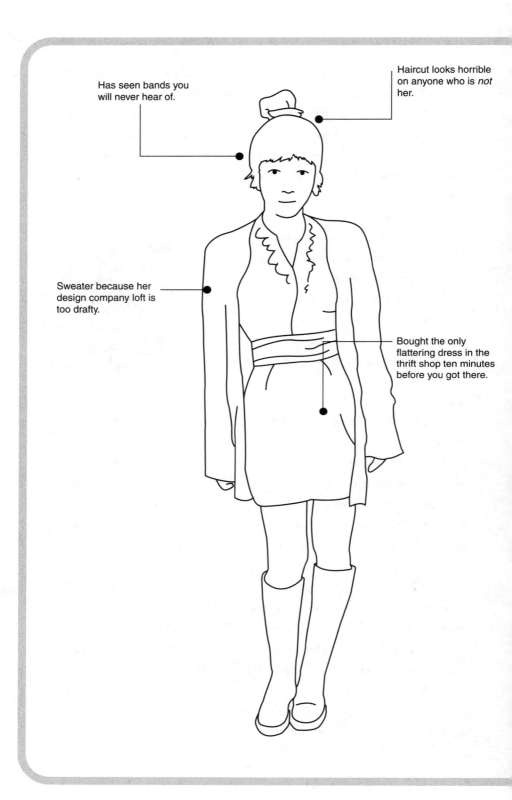

Has seen bands you will never hear of.

Haircut looks horrible on anyone who is *not* her.

Sweater because her design company loft is too drafty.

Bought the only flattering dress in the thrift shop ten minutes before you got there.

Montreal, Quebec

- **Overview** One of the more intimidating white people on the continent, the Montreal white person can speak perfect French and is probably in a band you haven't heard of yet. But you will.

- **Strengths** Can actually speak French.

- **Weakness** Crippling addiction to maple syrup. Also cigarettes.

- **Secret Shame** Once ate a bagel from New York and enjoyed it.

- **Second Secret Shame** Can't really speak French, just speaks gibberish around Americans and people from western Canada.

76 | Peacoats

As the temperature starts to drop, many white people are forced to start wearing winter coats. Though many will simply don outdoor performance gear, a great number will turn to the number-one white winter jacket of all time: the peacoat.

The peacoat was originally worn by sailors and members of the European navy. If you think about it for a second, this means that the coat is European, coastal, and vintage—three of white people's favorite things.

Another common characteristic of the coat is that white people will write their names on the label inside the coat. This is done not for fear of theft, but rather as a necessary precaution against party mix-ups. You see, when a white person attends a party in the wintertime they will often be required to put their jacket in a room with literally dozens of other peacoats! Since these coats often contain ticket stubs to the same concerts and identical Trader Joe's receipts, it can be impossible to find the original owner without a name written inside.

As is the case with sweaters, the process of acquiring a peacoat is almost as important as the coat itself. Fashionable white people can purchase designer peacoats for well over $1,000, but the highest-level white people purchase theirs at army surplus stores. This makes them feel better than the white people who have spent thousands of dollars on an identical piece of clothing.

Perhaps the greatest value of the peacoat is its ability to help you determine which nonwhite people have been accepted into the ranks of white people. It is not known if the coat is given to them in an elaborate ceremony or if they buy it themselves, but in either case by wearing the coat they are telling the world that they have white friends.

Long story short: if you want to increase your popularity with white people this winter, buy a peacoat.

77 *Vice* Magazine's Dos and Don'ts

Every white person has at least one book published by *Vice* magazine on their coffee table, bookshelf, or toilet tank. The most popular is *Vice's* book of fashion dos and don'ts. It is hilarious, and racist only some of the time.

The idea is simple: for the Dos section editors take photos of people who they think are cool and give them compliments. For the Don'ts section the editors take pictures of unsuspecting people, then black out their faces and make rude comments about what they are wearing. This is extremely popular because making fun of people behind their backs has been a part of white culture for thousands of years.

If you want to get a legendary buzz going around the office, you should say that your uncle was featured in the Don'ts section in 2001. This rumor will spread fast, so it's best to make sure that you have picked someone who matches up with you ethnically. If the caption is racist, then you can get whatever you want from any white person who finds it funny.

You might even be able to get a day off while everyone else goes through mandatory sensitivity training.

78 | Expensive Jeans

When it comes to clothing, there is nothing in white culture that is more justified than a nice pair of jeans. Aside from hippies, it is almost impossible for a white person to spend less than $100 on a pair of jeans. If it is a woman then that number triples to $300.

There is no room for argument on this one: expensive jeans are an absolute must for both work and social spheres. Wearing cheap jeans would instantly get them branded as the wrong kind of white people or, worse, as being like their parents. And while you might think that white people could turn to vintage jeans, you would be wrong. This is because white people can justify any piece of used clothing provided it never touched anyone's genitals. A used T-shirt that smells like onions and a wet dog? No problem; throw it in the wash—good as new. But a pair of used jeans? To a white person this prospect is on par with someone offering them a free installation of pubic lice.

Simply put, for white people expensive jeans are not a privilege, they are a right. Never is this more evident than at an antipoverty protest or a rally to raise money for an impoverished country. These events often feature a combined denim value that could probably wipe out the national debt of a small African country.

Also of note: White people wash their jeans, on average, two times a year while wearing their favorite pair, on average, five days a week.

79 Expensive Versions of Cheap Food

If you are looking for a small-business idea or you just need to cook a meal that will make white people happy, you can never go wrong making a very expensive version of something that is normally cheap food.

For example, many fancy restaurants have started offering gourmet hamburgers made with grass-fed organic prime beef topped with expensive cheese and onions and maybe truffles, served on brioche rolls. Additional examples include expensive hot dog carts, fancy cupcake shops, and restaurants offering $20 versions of macaroni and cheese.

While the concept of taking a type of food that is normally enjoyed by poor people and then making it prohibitively expensive can be seen as an "insult" or "giant middle finger" to poverty, white people don't see it that way.

Instead white people view these foods as a clever take on an old classic. Or in other words, it allows them to enjoy the food that would get them branded as the wrong kind of white person if they were to profess a love for it in a group setting.

For example, "I love Twinkies" would be met with scorn and derision. But saying something like "Oh my God, have you tried the new dessert at Delicieux? It's whipped heavy cream injected into this amazing masa cake. They call it 'An Evil Twinkie,' get it?" would result in a mad dash for reservations.

White people will often refer to these dishes as "comfort food." Because there are few things more comforting to white people than paying $14.99 for a grilled cheese.

Perfect White Party Games

- **Sufjan-ize a State** Come up with a funny title for a state you would like to see "Sufjan'd."

  "Oregon with the Wind"
  "I Nevada Chance"
  "Why oh Wyoming"

- **Ice Test** Say the words "All right, stop, collaborate, and listen" and wait for white people to fill in the rest.

- **Well-Read** Write down the names of famous or popular novels. Put them into a hat and draw one. Read it out and have each white person write down what they think happened in the plot. Less a party game, and more of what actually happens at white parties.

- **Seven Minutes in Heaven** White people are selected, then put into a dark closet with expensive headphones, vinyl reissues, and a glass of wine.

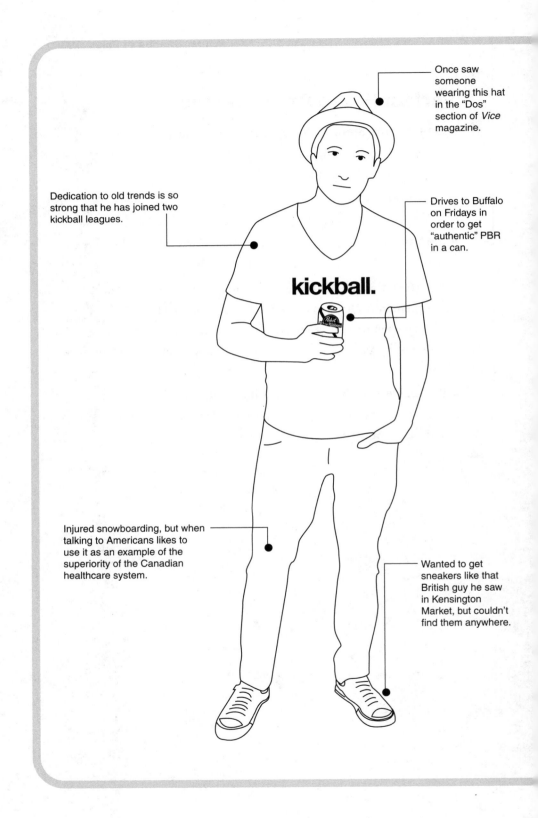

Once saw someone wearing this hat in the "Dos" section of *Vice* magazine.

Dedication to old trends is so strong that he has joined two kickball leagues.

Drives to Buffalo on Fridays in order to get "authentic" PBR in a can.

kickball.

Injured snowboarding, but when talking to Americans likes to use it as an example of the superiority of the Canadian healthcare system.

Wanted to get sneakers like that British guy he saw in Kensington Market, but couldn't find them anywhere.

Toronto, Ontario

- **Overview** The Toronto white person is urban and stylish, and you could say that they are exactly like the New York white person . . . of three years ago.

- **Strengths** Well traveled; can sort of speak French.

- **Weaknesses** City bylaw forces all residents to like Rush.

- **Secret Pride** Saying they are Canadian in Europe.

- **Secret Shame** Saying they are Canadian in New York.

80 Playing Children's Games as Adults

By far the easiest way to befriend a large group of white people is to organize and then participate in a game that is normally played by children. Unlike the practice of having their parents help with rent, this activity is a pleasant reminder to white people that they have not fully severed their ties with childhood.

When it comes to outdoor games, the most popular one remains kickball. In fact, you might have noticed groups of white people at the park playing this game in loosely organized leagues. Though kickball is certainly the most popular, if you were to suggest a game of Capture the Flag, Red Rover, British Bulldog, Tag, or even Hide and Go Seek, your popularity with white people would skyrocket. In addition, you would likely become a legend in your office.

White people are so happy to be outside reliving their childhood that they will all be in a good mood before the game even begins. But if you want to take it to the next level, you should have a friend show up and say to one of the white people, "Excuse me, what are you people doing?" The white person will tell them what game they are playing and promptly issue an invitation. To which your friend should say, "I'm sorry, I'm an adult. You people are crazy." It will make the white person feel great and give them a story to tell for years to come.

If you do not know enough white people for a large outdoor game or do not have access to adequate space, you are not out of luck. White people are also quite fond of indoor activities, especially ones that can be easily combined with alcohol. Therefore it is a rock-solid guarantee that you will gain white friends if you suggest a social gathering where people drink and play old board games like Candy Land, The Game of Life, or Mouse Trap. Just the suggestion of an event like this will get them more excited than word of a new Trader Joe's opening.

It's a good idea to space these events out lest you become "that weird guy who always wants to play Fireball Island."

81 Punctuality

If you have any experience making plans with white people, you already know they are very serious about being on time. In fact, they are so serious about it that they often show up early. If you tell a white person to meet you at 7 P.M., they will be there at 6:55 P.M.

If you have ever shown up late for an appointment with a white person, you likely believe that they are very understanding and laid-back people when it comes to punctuality. Nothing could be further from the truth.

On average, white people will complain about your rudeness once every thirty seconds beyond the agreed-upon meeting time. If they are alone they will complain to other friends via email or text message; if they are with another white person they will talk back and forth about how rude you are for wasting their time. When you finally arrive, they will act as though nothing is wrong, and no matter how late you show up, they will still pretend everything is fine!

This ability to pretend everything is fine even though they are filled with anger and hate is one of the most important skills for survival in a white family. You learn at a young age that disagreement and confrontation will lead to fights and, worse, elimination from the will.

"You're right, Grandpa, immigrants *are* destroying this country. How many square feet is this place again?"

If you want to reduce some of the built-up aggression, just tell the white person, "I'm sorry about being late. I'm on [insert ethnicity] time." This will make white people feel as though they have been let in on an ethnic joke, like when they watch a Chris Rock comedy special.

82 | Waiting in Line

When you see a long line of nonwhite people waiting for food, it is often the sign of a tragic event: communism, food shortages, or mismanagement by a dictator. When you see a line of white people waiting for food, it is the sign of a good bakery or concept restaurant.

Though you view waiting in line for food to be emblematic of all that is wrong with the world, white people see it as a small price to pay for a top-notch cupcake.

After years of waiting in lines for bakeries, concept restaurants, and ethnic restaurants with online buzz, white people have simply become accustomed to waiting in line. So much so that if they see a line near their intended destination they will simply move to the back and begin waiting. Additionally, white people will get in the line without asking anyone if they are in the right line. To ask if they're in the correct line would possibly give them away as someone who doesn't know what they are doing, or worse, as a first-time customer.

If you have a friend with a restaurant and you'd like to see his new business succeed, simply follow this plan. The first step is to get a few friends to wait in line in front of the restaurant. Ideally these would be white friends, but Asian friends are also acceptable. (For some reason Asians are also willing to wait ungodly amounts of time for food. Also, white people find a line of Asian people to be comforting.) Once you have assembled this line, simply wait for about thirty minutes. Any white person that walks by will instinctively just fall in line and wait for their turn to eat.

Of course, after they have waited in line for an hour, any food consumed will taste as though it's the finest meal they've ever eaten. So their reviews will be considerably higher than if they had just walked in off the street.

But before you start joining white people in line for just about any-

thing, you should understand that there are a lot of rules. The first is that white people take extreme pleasure in watching someone attempt to cut to the front of the line only to be rebuffed and sent to the back. This will make their entire day. On the flip side of that, watching someone successfully cut the line can lead to the closest approximation of a white person riot. Which is defined as fifteen people mumbling to each other and one particularly bold white person saying something sarcastic like "Yeah, that's right, we're just waiting in line for fun."

Entire outfit is simple, basic yoga wear. Retail value: $1,800.

Happy expression comes from spending forty hours a week on exercise, therapy, and natural medicine procedures. Also from spending zero hours a week working.

Fear of Western medicine leaves the Vancouver white person vulnerable to tetanus and lockjaw.

Vancouver, British Columbia

- **Overview** The Vancouver white person is considered by many to be the most elite white person on the whole West Coast. They have out-yogaed Los Angeles, out-Asian-fetished San Francisco, and out-outdoored Seattle. All three are nearly impossible tasks and yet Vancouver has been able to pull them off! The Vancouver white person can often be found engaging in any number of activities from Pilates to camping to drinking on a patio. In fact, the only activity you won't find them engaging in is work.

- **Strengths** Able to survive in the woods for up to two days on little more than $3,000 worth of equipment.

- **Weaknesses** Consecutive days of sunshine will leave a Vancouver resident disoriented.

- **Secret Shame** Bought dream catcher from online store and not from a real Native American.

83 | Taking a Year Off

When someone goes through a stressful experience they usually require some time off to clear their head, regain focus, and recover from the pain and suffering. Of course, in white culture these experiences are most often defined as finishing high school, making it through three years of college, or working for eleven months straight with only two weeks' vacation and every statutory holiday ("They don't count because I had to spend them with family").

Though you might consider finishing school or having a good job to be "accomplishments," many white people view them as burdens. As such, they can only handle them for so long before they start talking about their need to "take a year off" to travel, volunteer, or work abroad.

It is most common for the person taking the year off to use this time to travel. They start off with a set amount of money that they will live on for as long as possible. This explains why a white person with an $800 backpack will haggle with a poverty-stricken street vendor in a night market about a $2 plate of food.

If you work with this person, be sure to give them a *fake* email address on their last day on the job or you will be inundated with emails about spiritual enlightenment and how great the food is compared to similar restaurants back home. Also, within the first five days following departure, this person will come up with the idea to write a book about their travel experiences. Sadly, far more books about mid-twenties white people traveling have been written than have been read.

Some of the more enterprising white people will extend their time off by working abroad as a bartender, ski lift operator, or English teacher. Their stories, emails, and publishing plans will be identical to those of the previous white person but will include additional stories about work and complaints about "tourists."

Finally there is the white person who takes a year off to volunteer at home or abroad. Though they are equally likely to write long emails about their adventures, these people are often using the experience as an excellent résumé pad for their application to law school. This way they are able to put off real life without the crippling derailment of a career or education.

Regardless of how a white person chooses to spend their year off, they all share the same goal of becoming more interesting to other people. Sadly, the people who find these stories interesting are other white people who are politely listening until they can tell their own more interesting story about taking a year off.

Thankfully, there is an enormous opportunity for personal gain. You see, whenever a white person takes a year off it opens up a valuable apartment, job opportunity, or admissions slot. Consider it to be the most pretentious form of affirmative action.

84 Growing Their Own Food

Thanks to Michael Pollan and a number of frightening documentaries, more white people than ever are concerned about where their food comes from. Many white people have fantasies about opening their own organic farm where they could grow vegetables and herbs and potentially marijuana. But the reality of hard physical labor and living in a town with only one Thai restaurant is often enough to scare them straight. Instead many of them are choosing to plant small gardens at home.

When a white person gets it in their head that they are going to grow their own food, they will first justify it to themselves by calculating how much money they will save on basil if they grow it themselves. This is what is generally referred to as white person math. We have seen this before in the justification for the purchase of a kayak, the long-term value of liberal arts college tuition, and any trip to Whole Foods. Since white person math does not operate with any regard to logic or reason, it is not recommended that you inform a potential white farmer that the money they spend on gardening supplies will probably equal their yearly budget for vegetables.

Remember: You simply cannot put a price on the flavor enhancement that comes from self-satisfaction.

White people who do not have a yard will attempt to grow herbs in their small apartment. The top crop for white people in this situation is basil, followed by oregano, and then rosemary. Additionally, all white people will also go through a short-lived experiment with growing their own cilantro.

Ultimately it is strongly recommended that you befriend this white person, since they are the most likely to yield a free meal. Do not worry about the meal being low quality; no white person has successfully grown enough food for a full high-quality meal since the nineteenth century.

85 The Winter Olympics

It is guaranteed that white people will be the most competitive in environments where they compete exclusively against other white people: law schools, private school applications, conversations about music, and, of course, the Winter Olympics.

It's not that white people are afraid to compete against nonwhite people; it's just that were they to win they would be filled with an enormous sense of guilt that they only won because of the inherent advantage afforded them by their upbringing. Actually, forget that, they just don't like losing and so they invented the Winter Olympics.

After realizing in the Summer Olympics that it didn't cost anything to be a runner, white people decided they needed to do what they do best: make something open to everyone but prohibitively expensive so that only white people can compete. It worked for documentary filmmaking. Why wouldn't it work for sports?

And work it did. Now white athletes who aren't very good at running can be Olympic athletes in such costly sports as skiing, snowboarding,

and luge. Of course, there is figure skating, but much like the math department at an Ivy League school, it's an exception reserved mostly for Asians and Russian child prodigies.

Over the past few years, the Winter Olympics have expanded to make sure there's a sport for everyone to watch. Regular-level white people will stick to the classics like downhill skiing, pairs figure skating, and hockey. But for many years there were no sports that provided white people with the ironic thrill they need to truly enjoy it.

Then they added curling.

The addition of chubby Canadians, strange-panted Norwegians, mustachioed Americans, surprisingly attractive Swedes, and angry Brits provided white people with a sport they could truly call their own.

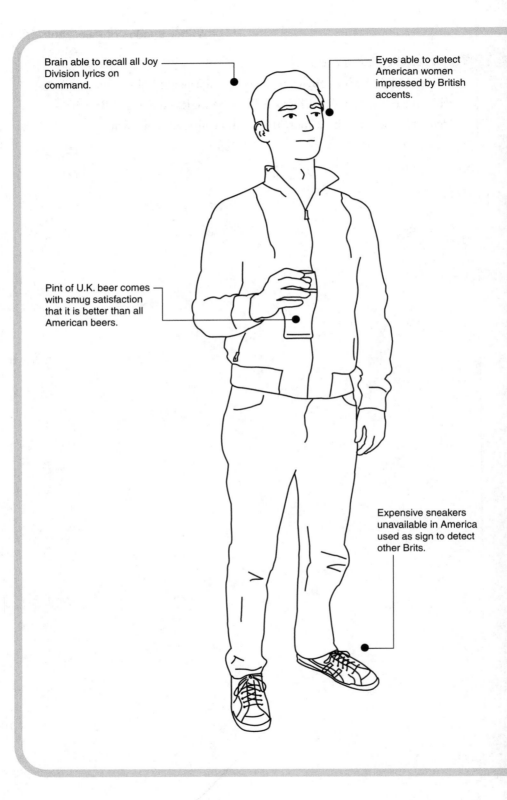

Brain able to recall all Joy Division lyrics on command.

Eyes able to detect American women impressed by British accents.

Pint of U.K. beer comes with smug satisfaction that it is better than all American beers.

Expensive sneakers unavailable in America used as sign to detect other Brits.

United Kingdom

- **Overview** British white people are considered one of the more advanced groups of white people on earth. They are like Canadians except that they have style, history, and relevance. British white people are also highly prized in the white world for their accents.

- **Strengths** Accent will attract opposite sex outside of the U.K.

- **Weaknesses** Relationships between white British people and non-white people have not ended well (see Wars, Opium, and Colonialism for further details).

- **Secret Shame** Once used the word *soccer*.

86 | *The Office*

Of television shows for white people, there are few more perfect than *The Office*. It's a smart comedy that shoots in a documentary style (something white people already like). The U.S. version features not one but two former members of *The Daily Show*, as well as a number of darlings of the indie comedy scene, and it's all overseen by white person hero Ricky Gervais. It goes without saying that this show is beloved by white people, but to put it over the edge and make it truly legendary it features one miracle trump card: a British edition.

You see, when white people have a choice between the British edition and the American edition they will always, without fail, choose the British. It's like how they will always say the book was better than the movie, unless that movie is *Twilight*—then they will say that both were horrible. The reason white people like the British edition is not so much that it is superior to the American edition; it's  just harder to find. You would have to have a Netflix subscription (not a problem for white people) or actively seek out the episodes on obscure American cable channels. But more important, the British edition gives white people an opportunity to assert dominance over other white people.

"I love *The Office*."
"Me too! Kelly is my favorite character!"

"Oh, you were talking about the American edition, Yeah, it's okay, I guess. Did you like *Men Behaving Badly*?"

"With Rob Schneider?"

"[Sigh.]"

87 | Banksy

Keeping up with art is hard; trips to galleries and museums, enormous books, and costly biannual magazines are just a few of the many expenses you will incur during an attempt to stay current with art. While most of these things would actually attract more white people than dissuade them, the amount of work required to become and remain an expert on art is simply too much for the majority of white people.

Of course, there are exceptions, such as the people who have invested both their money and their lives in the appreciation of art: people with art history degrees. But as you have probably noticed, they have very little value to you or society. The latter is evidenced by their annual salary while the former may be determined on a person-by-person basis.

Currently the artist who is both cutting-edge and easy to keep up with is Banksy, and white people love him. He is anonymous, British, easy to understand, and he works in the medium of graffiti! This last bit is very important since all white people consider graffiti to be art when it looks like something other than a bunch of squiggles. In every other instance, they consider it vandalism.

As with any conversation involving white people about taste, you are walking into a potential minefield. However, art does not work the same way as indie music, where obscurity is valued.

Here's how it works: If you say your favorite artist is Vincent Van Gogh, M. C. Escher, or Claude Monet, you will appear as though your taste in art is derived entirely from college posters. This is unacceptable. Jean-Michel Conversely, if you list Jeff Koons, Laurie Anderson, Damien

Hirst, or Jean-Michel Basquiat, you'll look like you are trying too hard but don't really know what you are talking about. Chances are that white people will assume your art education consists entirely of biopics and looking up references from *Gossip Girl*.

Finally, if you list an artist on the bleeding edge whom white people have not heard of, they will immediately recognize you as a threat and dislike you. It is also a certainty that they will call you pretentious behind your back.

Needless to say, it's complicated. But Banksy is just right. He's just edgy enough to be outside the mainstream, but popular enough to be available in coffee table book form at Urban Outfitters. (Though if you spot this book on the coffee table of white people it is strongly recommended that you imply they got the book at the shop of an art museum and not at Urban Outfitters. This

will make the evening far more enjoyable for everyone.) If you find all this to simply be too much work and wish to ensure that white people will never speak to you about art again, there is an easy escape. Simply mention that your favorite artist is Thomas Kinkade and that you are in negotiations to purchase an original from the store in the mall. This will effectively end any friendship you have with a white person.

88 Being Offended

To be offended is usually a rather unpleasant experience, one that can expose a person to intolerance and cultural misunderstandings, and even evoke long-dormant emotional scars. Many people develop a thick skin and try to be offended only in the most egregious and awful situations. In many circumstances they can allow smaller offenses to slip by, since fighting them is a waste of time and energy. But white people, blessed with both time and energy, are not these kind of people. In fact there are few things white people love more than being offended.

Naturally, white people do not get offended by statements directed at white people. In fact they don't even have a problem making offensive statements about other white people (ask a white person about "flyover states"). As a rule white people strongly prefer to get offended on behalf of other people.

It is also valuable to know that white people spend a significant portion of their time preparing for the moment when they will be offended. They read magazines and books and watch documentaries all in the hope that one day they will encounter a person who will say something offensive. When this happens, they can leap into action with quotes, statistics, and historical examples. Once they have finished lecturing another white person about how it's wrong to use the term *black* instead of *African-American*, they can sit back and bask in the knowledge that they have made a difference.

White people also get excited at the opportunity to be offended about sexism and homophobia, both cases offering ample opportunities for lectures, complaints, graduate classes, lengthy discussions, and workshops. All of which do an excellent job of raising awareness among white people who hope to change their status from "not racist" to "super not racist."

The threshold for being offended is a very important tool for judging and ranking white people. Missing an opportunity to be outraged is like missing a reference to Derrida—it's social suicide with little hope for a recovery.

If you ever need to make a white person feel indebted to you, wait for them to mention a book, film, or television show that features a character who is the same race as you, then say, "The representation of [insert race] was offensive, and if you can't see that, well, you need to do some soul searching." After they return from their hastily booked trip to the land of your ancestors, they will be desperate to make it up to you. At this point it is acceptable to ask them to help you paint your house.

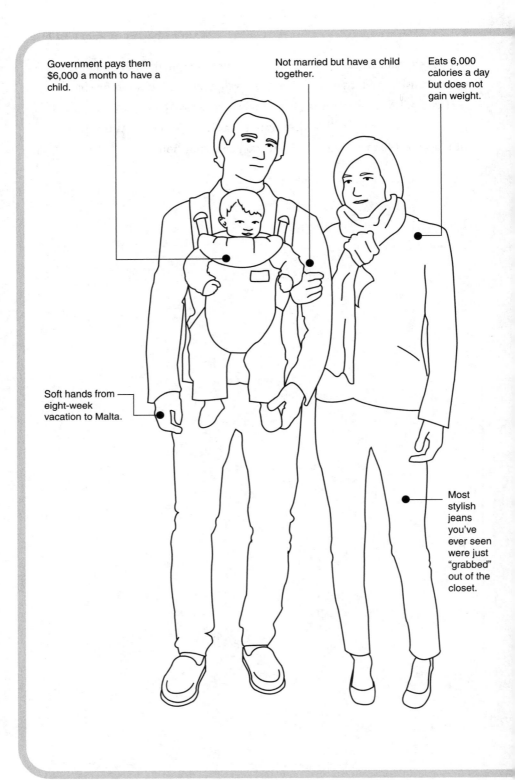

Government pays them $6,000 a month to have a child.

Not married but have a child together.

Eats 6,000 calories a day but does not gain weight.

Soft hands from eight-week vacation to Malta.

Most stylish jeans you've ever seen were just "grabbed" out of the closet.

Europe

- **Overview** Though Europe is filled with thousands of years of history, along with ethnic, religious, and nationalist conflicts, that all kind of blends together for North American white people. No, when a white person from North America thinks of Europeans, they think only of one thing: skinny.

- **Strengths** Currency; ability to wear slim-fit pants; six weeks of paid vacation.

- **Weaknesses** None are known.

- **Secret Shame** Techno.

- **Secret Pride** Techno.

89 Old Maps

The majority of things that white people put on their walls are easily explained: diplomas ("A degree in Eurasian studies *and* folklore? Impressive, kind of"), modern art ("This looks good next to your chair"), concert posters ("You saw that band before they got big; this poster pretty much proves that"), and personal photographs ("You went to Tibet twice?"). But there is a more puzzling piece of wall decoration that increasing numbers of white people are turning to: old maps.

You might think that white people like old maps because they are "vintage," and while you would be right, there is more to the story. Unlike art, posters, and degrees, it is very difficult for a white person to pass judgment on a map.

"Eighteen eighty-three New England? What is this, 1996? It's all about the St. Lawrence River this year."

This alone makes an old map very desirable. But it goes even deeper than that.

You see, every white person is nostalgic for time periods they never lived in. This is because they are convinced that if they'd lived in these periods, they would have been far more exceptional people than they are today. It's the same logic that Biff used in *Back to the Future Part II*, where he went back in time with a sports almanac and became superrich because he knew who to bet on. Though white people would prefer to believe that it is their intelligence and personality that would have made them a fantastic playwright, Cold War spy, senator, abolitionist, or muckraking journalist.

White people will generally choose maps based on the following criteria: Have I lived there? Have I traveled there? Is it hilariously out of date?

The latter is especially appealing to anyone who finds humor in the existence of Prussia or the Ottoman Empire (and for some reason, white people often do).

But in the end, white people like reminders of the past because it always has a happy ending. Either they would have had a sweet life, or they would have had an oppressed life that worked itself out in a generation or two. Perhaps this is why so many white people pursue degrees in history.

90 IKEA

If someone were to tell you that there was a large windowless store that provided an enormous amount of people with exactly the same mass-produced goods, you might think that they were describing some horrible Soviet-era furniture dispensary. In actuality, that store is IKEA and it is Swedish!

It is scientifically impossible to enter the home of a white person and not find at least one thing made by IKEA.

However, white people must be careful about how much they like IKEA. In fact, IKEA is a lot like taking cocaine recreationally: a lack of money in college only allows you to do it now and then, but when you start to get a little bit of money you have to work hard to fight the urge to let it take over your entire life.

When a white person receives a new IKEA catalog, they are first filled with a sense of elation as they think of replacing everything in their home to re-create the photographs of the beautifully lit European-style homes. To a white person a new IKEA catalog (or an extended trip to the website) is a bit like New Year's Day, in that they both inspire resolutions that will never be kept. "I'm going to get organized" or "The reason that I don't cook is because I hate my kitchen" are some popular ones.

But that joy quickly and inevitably turns to sadness as the white person realizes that all of their interior design hopes and dreams have been fabricated by a brilliant Swedish decorator. For many white people this process was sped up exponentially by that scene in *Fight Club* where Edward Norton realizes he has assembled the exact catalog. This is basically the white person equivalent of taking the red pill in *The Matrix*.

And yet still white people are unable to completely break free from this IKEA habit. They just learn to live with it, sort of like herpes. Currently the only people who are able to come close to breaking an IKEA addiction are those wealthy enough to shop at stores like Design Within Reach, or those with enough free time to cobble together a coherent living room from thousands of hours spent sifting through Craigslist and flea markets.

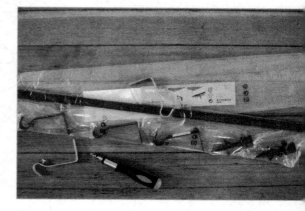

Outside the realm of furniture, IKEA also plays a very important role in determining the validity of a relationship between white people. When white people need to test if they can take their love any further as partners, they must take a trip to IKEA, where they will get into a fight. This is because all white couples get into fights at IKEA. It is currently unknown what causes the fights, though there is speculation that lingonberries trigger some sort of anger mechanism in the white brain.

In any case, if the white couple can survive the journey to IKEA then the relationship is strong enough for full domestic partnership.

In addition to providing you with cheap furniture, IKEA can also give you the perfect gift for a white person. Simply get them anything from the store and include a gift receipt. This is more personal than a gift certificate, and no white person will ever complain about having to go to IKEA to return their gift. They were headed there anyway.

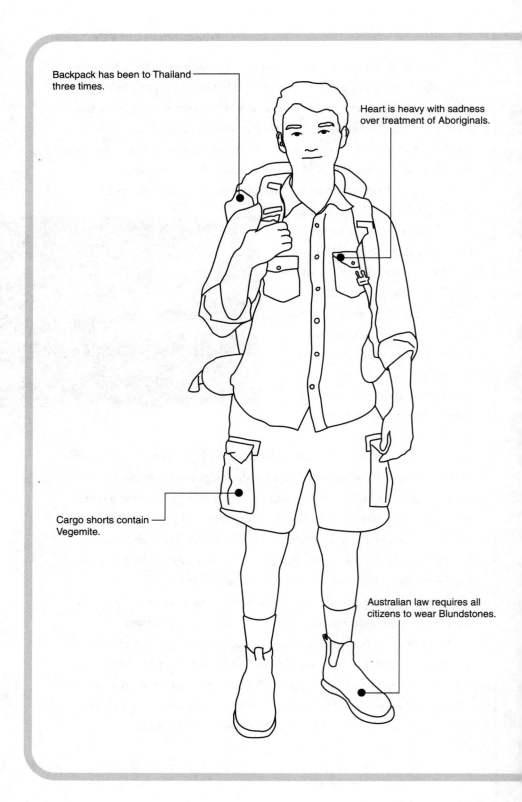

Backpack has been to Thailand three times.

Heart is heavy with sadness over treatment of Aboriginals.

Cargo shorts contain Vegemite.

Australian law requires all citizens to wear Blundstones.

Australia

- **Overview** Australians are a people who came to their land, displaced the natives, and now feel super guilty about it. In other words, they are just like North American white people but with a different accent and a few key vocabulary differences.

	America	Australia
Derogatory term for wrong kind of white person	Frat boy	Bogan
Term for those displaced by white people	Native American	Aboriginal
Term for architecture style that white people love	Victorian	Convict labour
Term for ancestor	Great-grandfather	Criminal
Term for New Zealander	Australian	New Zealander

- **Strength** Surfing ability; fun accent; sufficient ancestor guilt; capable of carrying enormous backpacks.

- **Weakness** Midnight Oil.

- **Secret Shame** Once used acccent to try and get free Bloomin' Onion at Outback Steakhouse in Tampa, Florida.

91 | Thailand

Throughout history, leaders of organized religion have always searched for ways to increase their number of followers and converts. Some have relied on force, others on charity, and others simply on birthrates. Though it has never been confirmed, there are sneaking suspicions that Buddhist leaders created Thailand for the sole purpose of converting white people to Buddhism.

It is literally impossible for a white person to travel to Thailand and not return as a Buddhist. This conversion is a powerful experience, one that will result in a potential trip to a temple when they return home, maybe reading a few books, and the inevitable acquisition of a Buddha or a Buddha head. The latter of course is based on income and space available at home.

Buddhism meshes quite well with white people since they interpret the religion as a reaffirmation that everything they are doing is just great and they'll be fine in the afterlife. For a white person there is no better spiritual awakening than one that tells you that you were right all along. It's like taking a journey to find the meaning of life and when you get to the end there's a copy of your student film from college.

When white people are told that a key tenet of Buddhism is that all suffering is caused by desire, they understand immediately that they have been so depressed because they want that Eames chair that they can't afford. Finally religion is put into terms they can understand.

But with so many white people undertaking this identical journey, you would expect them to eventually realize that they are all taking the same trip. Yet no matter how many thousands of white people travel to Thailand each year, every person who makes the journey likes to believe they are the first Western eyes to ever see a crumbling Buddhist temple.

White people don't just come back from this spiritual journey with a taste for enlightenment; they also bring a taste for pad thai. Their two-week vacation was more than enough time for them to become experts on the national dish of the country, and within the white community they are given full rights to complain about any and all local Thai food being "watered down" for other white people's palates.

However, it should be noted that the passion white people have for Thai food is directed mostly to pad thai, curries, and dishes with ingredients they recognize. If you hear a white person telling you how much they love Thai food, do not take them for boat noodles or anything else that might contain tripe. Remember, white people like exotic foods, but not enough to eat something that might be gross.

Still, if you go out to eat with white people it is a certainty that you will end up at a Thai restaurant at some point. If you are familiar with actual Thai food, you might be surprised to see these Thai-loving white people eating their food with chopsticks. Under no circumstance should you ever point out that people in Thailand use forks and spoons. It will make the white person sad that no one on their trip told them, not even that nice man who tried to sell them a prostitute.

92 | Hipster Weddings

If you know a white couple under forty who have recently gotten married, there is a 100 percent chance they were involved in a "hipster" wedding. These affairs work almost identically to regular weddings, except the groom is wearing Chuck Taylor All-Stars instead of dress shoes.

White people choose this type of wedding for the same reason they choose almost anything: to be slightly different from their friends and to inspire at least a small amount of jealousy.

There are multiple areas in which white people can express their individuality in a wedding. Should you be invited to one of these events, the activity that will probably most surprise you is the entrance of the bride.

Ever since a video surfaced of a woman doing a coordinated dance down the aisle to a pop song, the imitators have been numerous. Because when they look back on this day, white people want to be reminded that they treated it with all the gravity and seriousness of an eighth-grade dance.

But do not judge white people for this; a look at white divorce rates shows that they are doing it not out of disrespect for the institution of marriage but as a self-defense mechanism. When a serious marriage fails it's crushing, but when a marriage that was more of an excuse for a photo shoot than a life together falls apart you move on.

Which brings us nicely to the next part of a white hipster wedding: the recording. Not only will the event be recorded via literally thousands of Hipstamatic iPhone photos of the bride and groom, but there will also be a professional photographer capturing everything. Keep in mind, though, that in white culture "professional photographer" means "family friend who needs some money."

Of course, no matter who takes the pictures, all of the photos look as though they were taken in the 1970s or earlier. Much in the same way that white people spend a lot of money to look poor, they will also spend a lot of money on exceptionally expensive photographic equipment to get results that look like they were taken with a thirty-year-old camera.

If there is a video component to the wedding, you can be assured that within two weeks of the wedding you will be sent a link to a Vimeo page to see a twenty-five-minute "film" that looks more like a David Lynch experiment than an actual wedding video.

Also, the importance of music cannot be overstated. If the groom is not a DJ or a music blogger, this will be his one chance to put together a legendary mix that will make his friends appreciate his taste in music. You should always compliment the groom on the music, but you should never say, "Okay, enough with this whiny stuff, when are we going to hear something you can dance to?" This is considered an insult.

If you choose to marry a white person, you should know that they will attempt to insert some or all of the aforementioned quirks into the wedding. It is essential that you tell them that your parents are insisting on a traditional affair. Even if you don't care too much for a traditional wedding, the hassles will be far less than trying to come to an agreement with your spouse on the appropriate theme for your wedding cupcakes.

White Shoes

- **Sperry Top-Siders** Comforting reminder that white people could be drinking wine on a boat at a moment's notice.

- **Chuck Taylor All-Stars** Worn by rock stars since the 1970s, almost impossible to use for any real sports other than kickball (not a problem for white people).

- **Birkenstock sandals** For more than thirty years these shoes have been associated with two things that are beloved by white people: academics and old lesbians.

- **Vans Slip-Ons** Rose to national prominence when they were worn by Sean Penn in *Fast Times at Ridgemont High* (it has been proven that white people will like anything Sean Penn tells them to).

Acknowledgments

There are a lot of people who have helped to make this book and the previous book possible. Without their help this would still be a goofy blog. First off I want to thank Myles Valentin, the genius and co-founder of the site. He is, without a doubt, the world's greatest expert on racial humor. I want to thank my wife, Jessica, for her fantastic photography and her brutal honesty in telling me when something is not funny. And of course I want to thank my whole family for serving as the greatest promotions unit on earth.

I want to thank Ron Calixto and Sean Owen for their tireless work in determining whether or not a post deserves to make it to the site or the book.

Of course, the book wouldn't exist without Random House. I owe so much of my success to my amazing editors, Jill Schwartzman and Ryan Doherty; to my fantastic publisher, Jane Von Mehren; and to the amazing publicity team of Barbara Fillon and Ashley Gratz-Collier. Additionally, neither book would have been possible without Becca Shapiro, Beth Pearson, Erich Schoeneweiss, Liz Cosgrove, Leigh Marchant, Greg Mortimer, Thomas Pitoniak, Evan Stone, Ben Steinberg, or Marisa Vigilante.

I would be lost without my agent, Erin Malone, and the William Morris Endeavor Agency.

The book looks fantastic thanks to the line drawings of Joel Eikenberry and Jason Wilkins, who also did an amazing job on designing a run of beautiful Stuff White People Like posters from their apartment in Arkansas. Thanks also to Alex Boeckl for his great work on the Stuff White

People Like T-shirts, which have been so helpful in raising money for Children of the Night.

I want to give a special thank-you to every college and bookstore that has ever allowed me to speak within its walls.

And last but not least, I want to thank every person who reads Stuff White People Like, every person who forwards a post to their friends, every person who writes in to the site, and every person who has ever created a spin-off site.

I can't believe I got to do this twice.

Illustration Acknowledgments

All line art by Joel Eikenberry and Jason Wilkins.

The numbers listed below refer to the entries (e.g., #1 is Ivy League).

iStockphoto@: 1, 2, 4, 5, 6, 7, 8, 9, 13, 16, 18, 19, 21, 30, 31, 32, 33, 35, 36, 38, 39, 40, 44, 46, 48, 50, 51, 53, 54, 56, 57, 61, 62, 64, 68, 74, 76, 77, 78, 81, 86, 87, 93

Jess Lander: 3, 10, 11, 14, 15, 17, 20, 22, 24, 26, 27, 28, 29, 42, 43, 45, 47, 49, 52, 55, 58, 59, 60, 63, 66, 67, 69, 70, 71, 75, 79, 80, 82, 83, 84, 85, 88, 89, 90, 91, 92

Jill Schwartzman: 12, 23, 25, 34, 37, 65, 72, 73

Matt Johannes: 23

Rebecca Shapiro: 41

Ryan Doherty: 30